WITHDRAWN

Get **more** out of libraries

Please return or renew this item by the last date shown.

You can renew online at www.hants.gov.uk/library

Or by phoning 0845 603 5631

5/13

Hampshire
County Council

JULIA CASTERTON

First published in 2005 by
The Crowood Press Ltd
Ramsbury, Marlborough
Wiltshire SN8 2HR

www.crowood.com

British Library Cataloguing-in-Publication Data
A catalogue record for this book is available from the British Library.

ISBN 1 86126 748 7

Typeset by Jean Cussons Typesetting, Diss, Norfolk

Printed and bound in Great Britain by MPG Books, Bodmin, Cornwall

CONTENTS

DEDICATION

This book is dedicated to all the poets who have gone before, whether or not we know their names, who have given the vital part of themselves, their imagination, to keep poetry alive and so keep the world in tune with itself, whatever the chaos and dissonance that surrounded them. It is dedicated to all the poets who are writing now, who make poems for no payment, against the pressures of other work, making delight and meaning in a world that sometimes seems to contain neither. It is also dedicated to you, the reader, who have decided to join the visionary company, to begin to re-enchant the world so that we might save it.

WHY POETRY?
A PRETEXT

I am imagining you. You have just walked into a bookshop, or a library, and opened this book. Perhaps you opened it because you have written a few poems already, and you want to find out more about how poetry works. But somewhere in your mind there's a feeling, a question, a doubt: why do I want to write poems? Why not a novel or a screenplay? Or why don't I just graffiti the Town Hall?

In ancient times, all forms of writing were poems. Our earliest stories (the *Epic of Gilgamesh*, the Bible, the *Iliad* and the *Odyssey*, the *Tao Te Ching*, the Indian and Buddhist scriptures) come to us in the form of poetry. They have rhythms, sometimes rhymes, and tunes. Some of them were sung to the lyre, and so were called lyric poetry. So this may be the first reason you want to write poems: to return to the sources of writing, to find the fresh places from which it originally sprang.

These sources are in yourself too. Your first experience of language may have been the insistent rhythms that came to you through nursery rhymes:

One misty moisty morning
When cloudy was the weather
I chanced to meet an old man
Clothed all in leather

or

Inky pinky ponky
Daddy bought a donkey
Donkey died
Daddy cried
Inky pinky ponky

The first one gives you the mysterious limping rhythm of the iambic metre (an iamb, in ancient Greek, is a lame man) and the second the energetic, bursting rhythm of the trochaic metre, which literally means 'the running foot'. So if you heard nursery rhymes as a child, you were already, before you even knew it, steeped in the two most popular poetic metres. Poetry entered into you before you could even speak. This could be the second reason you want to write poems: because the poems are inside you, and want to come out.

You may be coming to poetry out of a sense of loss. Many people take great delight in listening to, and making poems, but school or university or work seem to squeeze that joy out of you, and you want to discover again the 'heaven' that 'lies about us in our infancy' that Wordsworth wrote about. As poems are close to music, close to dance, and, paradoxically, close to silence, they can lead you out of the deadened feeling of loss that arises when you have to do work, whether manual or intellectual, that alienates you from your deepest self, and take you back to the beloved, the stranger who is the eternal part of yourself.

Or perhaps you are angry. You have been dishonoured in some way that threatens your very essence, and you need to stand up for yourself. You feel that if you don't stand up for yourself you will go under, to paraphrase the German poet and playwright Bertolt Brecht. Well, there is a strong tradition of anger, protest and speaking bitterness in poetry. Poems to change the world are made by all peoples who suffer injustice and indignity. Napoleon said that *La Marseillaise* was worth more than a whole regiment of cavalry: poems and songs are ammunition in the war against tyranny. They also heal the hearts of those who compose them, and those who hold them in their minds.

You may have an illness, something inside that is causing you harm, and you want to get it down on to paper. If you attend to the wounded places in yourself – tunefully, rhythmically, discovering the timbre of your own voice and its changing dynamics – a feeling of well-being will gradually arise. All forms of creativity play a part in healing, but poems take up very little space and can be composed anywhere, so they can claim a prime place in the self-healer's strategy.

Or perhaps you have come to this book because you simply want to be published. You have been writing poems for a while and you want to see them in print. This is an admirable ambition, albeit one that people often keep hidden for many years. 'Fame is the spur' said Gerard Manley Hopkins, who had no poetry published during his own lifetime, even though we now consider him to be one of the founders of modern poetry. Whenever I read one of his breathtaking poems, I consider how much more wonderful verse he could have written if he had experienced the encouragement of being published. Publication helps the poet continue to write, and it is vital if you are to communicate with an audience beyond your own circle. Indeed, poetry, when it succeeds, enables you to communicate with those who are not yet born – which in a way, brings a form of immortality.

Perhaps all poems are written by those who are most afraid of dying and disappearing without trace, those who want to leave something of themselves behind. This is certainly true for me. I love being alive and, while not consciously afraid of dying, I am aware while writing each poem that it contains my own stamp or signature, my 'I was here' message for when I leave.

But underneath all the reasons for writing poems is a particular feeling, one we call delight. You may not feel it at first. There could be too much dark material preventing you bringing it to the surface and setting it loose on paper. But soon you will feel a lightening. The dark material leaves your mind and your body and appears on the screen or the paper, where you can look at it, stand back, see what works and what does not in what you have written. It's no longer part of you; it has its own reality. You can see your own clichés and sentimentality, think 'That's awful!' and cross it out. You can find the parts of yourself that are more interesting and write those instead. The poet Rainer Maria Rilke said that everything is about praise, and he was right. It all comes down to praise in the end. You may begin with a curse, but the poems will make it come out differently.

There are many reasons for writing poems, and your own reasons may well be different from those I have described. No matter. If you feel drawn to poetry, work your way through the exercises in this book. They will give you a thorough grounding in the different genres of poetry, its wonderful variety of forms, metres, textures, melodies, timbres and rhymes. In exploring all these possibilities, you will discover more about your own unique writing voice, and more about why you need to write poems.

1 THE ORIGINS OF POETRY

We know when people began to write novels. We know when cinema started. But poems – when did they begin to be written? And were they composed orally long before they were written down?

The Australian poet Les Murray suggested that poets are paid so little in comparison with novelists and screenwriters precisely because their art is so very ancient. Poets made poems long before the idea of money ever crossed anyone's mind. They were given a good meal, a laurel crown or perhaps even the king's ring by way of thanks for a poem commemorating a battle won or a royal wedding – and the habit has persisted. Poets, even the most famous ones, sell surprisingly few volumes of their poetry. They make their livings through modern forms of patronage: prizes, bursaries, employment in institutions of learning, being appointed a poet laureate. Or at least the ones who have become respectable do. There are others: advertisers, performers, rebels, drunks, secret writers, who scavenge around in the mire of the world and write poems that attack the status quo. They rarely get paid for their poems but they write them anyway. They have to. As do the ones who have become respectable.

And the two worlds overlap. The respectable poets may look down on the rebels and the rebels show contempt towards the respectable, but they cross over because they need each other. Just as the minor gentry need the racing gangs in order to maintain control over gambling. And poetry is the crime they are all committing: it is crime, because it cannot help but disclose what should not be disclosed, give away secrets, show contempt of court, scandalize the powerful. Poetry cannot truly be in anyone's pay, even though the poets themselves might gratefully accept the king's shilling. Because poetry is essential. It emerges from layers of consciousness that we know little about. Deep sources of wisdom and rectitude we may be unaware of, but which exist nevertheless. Our essence.

That is not to say that some poems don't lie. They do. You can spot lies in poems that are wilful tear-jerkers, sentimental in a manipulative way, or inauthentic. (We will examine this particularly when discussing war poetry in Chapter 4.) But in general, if you get to know a country's poets, you get to know the country. Poets are the bedrock, what lies beneath the lies. The origins. There is a poet in everyone, and perhaps everyone was once a poet.

I would like you now to think about the origins of your own fascination with poetry, and also with song. Out of this you will write your first poem – or the first poem, anyway, that emerges out of your reading of this book.

YOUR FIRST SONG

Unplug the telephone and open the window. This is your own time, not to be invaded. Give yourself an hour. An hour away from your normal obligations isn't going to hurt anyone, and it will do you enormous good.

Find a comfortable place to sit, with your back well-supported. Breathe deeply, and think about nothing but your breath, taking it in and letting it go. This is a way of getting rid of all the irritating buzzing that mostly occupies your mind: the obligations, to-do lists, bits of guilt and remorse that stand in the way of creative work. Concentrating on the breath gently quietens the buzzing, so allow yourself at least five minutes of empty time, just breathing, to get yourself ready for the poem that is going to come.

When your breathing is steady and your mind clear, allow yourself to begin to think about the songs, poems and rhymes you first heard, the poetry of your earliest memories. Close your eyes. This will enable you to go back to that time more easily. As you shut out the objects of the present, you open the door to the treasure-house of the past. Continue to listen, though, to sounds: birdsong, people talking in the street, drills – any of these could trigger a memory which will set the poem moving inside you.

After a while stray words and fragments of tune will begin to surface. What are the words? Hold them in your mind. Are they harsh and dissonant, or sweet and harmonious? Or both? How do they make you feel? Or are they pure sound, the sounds that come before words? Although the Bible says 'In the beginning was the Word', D.H. Lawrence replied, in his wonderful travel book *Mornings in Mexico* (1927), 'In the beginning was the chirrup' because in the morning there the birds brought him such pleasure. Your own memories might take you back to a pre-verbal world, before things were given names, where there were sounds, smells, textures, tastes and sights, but no words for them yet. Let yourself enter fully into the world of the poem.

Now move over to your desk or table, and pick up your pen. Allow it to move over the page without thinking. If you get stuck, and nothing's coming, then put your pen in the other hand. Write with the hand you don't normally use. This enables you to make contact with parts of your mind that are usually inaccessible to you. What you write then will surprise you. Write for five minutes. Anything. Anywhere on the page. Don't try to write sentences if they don't come naturally. Single words. Phrases. Whatever comes is right.

When you have written as much as you want to write, slowly bring yourself back to the everyday world. Come back to your breathing (*in – out – in – out*). Breathing consciously means being fully alive. It's no accident that our word

The words 'Ride a cock-horse to Banbury Cross' were as haunting to me, who did not know then what a cock-horse was nor cared a damn where Banbury Cross might be, as, much later, were such lines as John Donne's, 'Go and catch a falling star, Get with child a mandrake root,' which also I could not understand when I first read them. And as I read more and more, and it was not all verse, by any means, my love for the real life of words increased until I knew that I must live *with* them and *in* them always. I knew, in fact, that I must be a writer of words, and nothing else. The first thing was to feel and know their sound and substance; what I was going to do with those words, what use I was going to make of them, what I was going to *say* through them, would come later. I knew I had to know them most intimately in all their forms and moods, their ups and downs, their chops and changes, their needs and demands ...

Let me say that the things that first made me love language and want to work *in* it and *for* it were nursery rhymes and folk tales, the Scottish Ballads, a few lines of hymns, the most famous Bible stories and the rhythms of the Bible, Blake's *Songs of Innocence*, and the quite incomprehensible magical majesty and nonsense of Shakespeare heard, read, and near-murdered in the first forms of my school.

Dylan Thomas, 'Notes on the Art of Poetry', *The Texas Quarterly* (1961)

for breathing is inspiration, or that a word for dying, for our final breathing-out, is 'to expire'. The in-breath takes everything in and the out-breath cleanses us of the things we don't need.

What you have done in this first writing exercise is to take a gigantic in-breath, by writing down everything you can remember about the origins of poetry which are inside yourself. A little later we will come to the next stage, where you find your way to constructing a poem from the marks you have just made on the page. But for now, after you've had a look at it, put it away, in a drawer or in a box. Let it sit there for a while (and sit in your mind too) while we spend some time exploring some of the things that were written in ancient times: the poems our far ancestors wrote and why they wrote them.

THE SONGS THE ANCIENTS SANG

Imagine the lives of our earliest forebears. They were vulnerable to the weather, the dark, and attack from other human beings or wild animals. They moved around in search of food, and to supplement their hunting they ate roots, leaves, fruit and berries, some of which were poisonous or caused frightening hallucinations. As they learned to live in the world perhaps they were often afraid and longed for something to keep them steady, to help them keep their nerve while they started to feel at home here. What could give them that feeling of belonging?

A fire built for protection at night might have given them comfort. And no one has ever been able to leave a fire alone. It calls to you, with its crackling sounds, its constantly changing colours, its nourishing heat. Our forebears will surely have been drawn to sit around it, to gaze into it and, in its warmth, to gaze out into the night and up at the stars. Their minds may have wandered – towards the beings that could be out there, who might be available to protect them or guide them. Should they try to talk to these beings, sing to them, dance for them? Remember, there was no television to interrupt them and bring their thoughts to everyday matters. Their minds could go wherever they wanted, without the irritation of adverts or the news.

Some of the most ancient poems are Sanskrit chants which invoke the gods, offer them salutations and ask for protection from harm and healing from sickness. Some chants also seek to make benign connections between the earthly and the heavenly realms, to build bridges between human beings and the gods.

Madame Blavatsky, who was a mentor to the poet W.B. Yeats, said that the gods prefer to be addressed in their own language, which is Sanskrit. Whether or not this is true, Sanskrit is the mother of many languages, and you may find, when trying out some of the chants, that you feel at home in them even though you don't understand the words. What I want you particularly to be aware of is the vowels. As you intone a chant with lots of 'aaaahhhh' sounds, see how different it feels, inside your throat and inside your whole body, from a chants which contain more 'eeee' or 'oooohhhh' or 'uuuuu' sounds.

A selection of chants can be found in Thomas Ashley-Farrand's *Healing Mantras* (Gateway Press, 2000), and I have chosen two of these to illustrate the sounds used and their effects.

Here is the first mantra, which I would like you to try intoning out loud (the pronunciation is shown underneath) and see how it makes you feel. Chant it twenty times.

Om Dum Durgayei Namaha
AUM DOOM DOOR-GAY-YEI NAHM-AH-HA

You may have noticed that the rather closed 'uuuu' sounds give way, in the middle of 'Durgayei', to more open 'aaayyy' sounds, and that these themselves then expand further into the truly generous 'aaahhh' sounds at the end.

The mantra is in fact an invocation of Durga, who is a goddess of protection. She rides a lion or a tiger and has a hundred arms, each with a different weapon to defeat any force that tries to harm her followers. The open sound at the end ('Namaha') means 'salutations'. When you chant this mantra you are offering salutations to an ancient feminine protective force.

Although in Western societies we tend to believe that a word holds an arbitrary relationship to its meaning, nevertheless it is possible to create, by the sounds of our words, the feelings we want to convey. Some words take us closer to their meaning or essence than others. Take this mantra, for example:

Om Arkaya Namaha
AUM AHR-KAY-YAH NAHM-AH-HA

It means 'Om and salutations to the Shining One who removes afflictions' and is an invocation of the healing power of the sun. Listen to the way 'Om' (which means 'the beginning of all things made and all things not made') seems to leap up, with the word 'Arkaya' in a giant curve to reach the healing source, and then return to earth again with 'Namaha', the word that salutes the sun.

You can feel the powerful effect of the sound of the words, too, in John Keats's sonnet 'To Sleep'. Here are the opening lines:

O soft embalmer of the still midnight
Shutting with careful fingers and benign
Our gloom-pleased eyes, embowered from the light,
Enshaded in forgetfulness divine ...

Can you see the way he repeats his vowels, sometimes in a slightly different form, to spread and stretch them out so that the words feel very long and languorous, as though they themselves were sleepy? So 'still' is followed by 'midnight', the 'i' lengthening over the two words, and the same with 'fingers' and 'benign'. You can stretch your vowels to slow the whole poem down, and you can shorten them if you want to make the poem move fast, as W.H. Auden did in his famous poem 'Night Mail'.

This is the Night Mail crossing the border,
Bringing the cheque and the postal order.
Letters for the rich, letters for the poor,
Letters for the butcher and the girl next door.

The short vowels, combined with an insistent dactylic metre (one strong beat followed by two weak ones), give the verse an urgent forward movement which is exactly right for the subject matter.

I'd like you now to try your own 'Hymn to the Gods'. It doesn't matter if you don't believe in anything beyond the material world. Think of what you love most (a person, a kind of food, a tree, money) and write a hymn to that. But don't write it in English first off. Write it in the language you think your god would most like to hear. Make up the language: six lines in an unknown language to salute your god. I am asking you to do this so you will be free to write sounds without meaning, so you can get the feeling for yourself of the moods sounds can produce on their own, even when they are not bound up with what things mean.

When you have written your Hymn in your invented language, translate it into English, but be sure to stay true to the mood you created by keeping some of the same sounds. As you know, in principle, it's the way we say and write something that creates the emotional effect, rather than simply *what* we say.

12

Sentence Sounds

The ear does it. The ear is the only true writer and the only true reader. I have known people who could read without hearing the sentence sounds and they were the fastest readers. Eye readers we call them. They can get the meaning by glances. But they are bad readers because they miss the best part of what a good writer puts into his work.

Remember that the sentence sound often says more than the words. It may even as in irony convey a meaning opposite to the words.

I wouldn't be writing all this if I didn't think it the most important thing I know. I write it partly for my own benefit, to clarify my ideas for an essay or two I am going to write some fine day (not far distant).

To judge a poem or piece of prose you go the same way to work – apply the one test – greatest test. You listen for the sentence sounds. If you find some of those not bookish, caught fresh from the mouths of people, some of them striking, all them definite and recognizable, so recognizable that with a little trouble you can place them and even name them, you know you have found a writer.

Robert Frost, *Selected Letters*, ed. Lawrence Thompson (Holt, Rinehart and Winston, 1964)

When you've written your second poem, look at it briefly and then put it away, as you did the first. We'll do more work on them at the end of the chapter.

ANCIENT WISDOM

When we read the oldest poems, we come into contact with the original questions that human beings asked about being in the world, about how we should behave, the mysteries of life and death and our connections with the forces that shape and guide our lives. The ancient poems provide us with strong sources of energy to address some of the most fundamental questions of our lives, so it's worth taking a look at some of them, to examine the answers our forebears came up with, and seeing how they compare with our own. If you don't know these poems, you may be surprised at the similarity of the wisdom they contain, and how different it is from what we, in modern secular societies, tend to think of as good sense.

In the *Bhagavad Gita* (literally, Song of the Lord), the god Krishna speaks to Arjuna, one of his favoured human subjects, about the way to attain happiness in life:

If you take delight in your own talents
you will attain perfection ...

It's better to do your own duty imperfectly
than do another's duty well ...

You should not abandon your own
natural-born action, even though it be faulty.
The faults will be dimmed, as fire is by smoke.

If you do not attach yourself to any object,
if you conquer yourself, and are free from longings,
you will reach, through renunciation,
the supreme perfection, which is without action.

Anon., Bhagavad Gita
(Harvard University Press, Cambridge, Mass., 1972), verses 45–50.
(The translation is a little archaic, so I have modified it somewhat.)

There are at least two things here for a poet to consider: that you should do what comes naturally to you, rather than forcing yourself on a path that goes against the direction of your essential self; and that you should let go of things and belongings. It is this emptying out, this state of receptive vacancy, that will most help you in your preparation for writing poems. Chanting and meditation can cleanse your mind of its irritating chatter, and enable you to discover the relaxed readiness that is the prime condition for any kind of creativity.

The Russian poet Osip Mandelstam believed that poems came to him from sources beyond his own mind, and that his task, as a poet, was to walk around saying them out loud until the dead wood, the words that were not essential for the poem, began to fall away. And Ted Hughes wrote about lying in wait for a poem, as one would for a wild animal. If they were right, then this patient, alert eagerness, where you expect nothing but simply are, in your own essence, waiting, is a state that will enable the poem to come to you.

The *Upanishads* are spiritual treatises, the oldest composed between 800 and 400BC. The word means 'sitting at the feet of a master', and they contain this listening quality, full of longing, that I've just mentioned. The opening of the *Kena Upanishad* enters straight into some of the original mysteries:

Who sends the mind to wander afar? Who first drives life to start on its journey? Who impels us to utter these words? Who is the Spirit behind the eye and the ear?

It is the ear of the ear, the eye of the eye, and the Word of words, the mind of mind, and the life of life. Those who follow wisdom pass beyond and, on leaving his world, become immortal.

There the eye goes not, nor words, nor mind. We know not, we cannot understand, how he can be explained: He is above the known and he is above the unknown ...

He comes to the thought of those who know him beyond thought, not to those who imagine he can be attained by thought ...

He is known in the ecstasy of an awakening which opens the door of
life eternal. By the Self we obtain power, and by vision we obtain Eternity.
Anon.

The Upanishads, *translated by Juan Masaro (Penguin, 1965)*

You may wonder at first: is this poetry? It contains no separate verses, no
regular rhythm or number of syllables: why is it a poem? This is a difficult
question to answer, as the boundaries between poetry and prose are beginning
to blur again, as they were blurred at the start of written language. It appears
that, when writing first appeared, everything, apart from the most basic
household accounts, was poetry. I think that it is because of the urgency of the
material being presented. Poetry grabs you by the scruff of the neck and makes
you sit still. The American poet Emily Dickenson described it as making you
feel as if the top of your head is coming off.

It may look like prose, but if it sounds like poetry, then it is poetry. If it
addresses fundamental human questions in a language that captivates you,
then it is coming from the deep sources of poetry.

A poem results from a poetic moment. That moment occurs when events,
images, feelings and ideas coalesce and fuse with one another. The moment
becomes a poem when the poet creates the words and phrases that best contain
its truths. The choosing of words and the creation of strings of phrases and their
arrangement become the form of the poem. The choices in this process are
aesthetic ones – of tone, intensity, movement, cadence and polyphony – for a
poem may depend on more than one stream of ideas and images. The truths of a
poem thus lie as much in the emotional and aesthetic as in the cerebral. Its power
lies in the spell it casts upon the reader. This in turn is the criterion for its
successful accomplishment.

Judy Gahagan, Letters (unpublished)

It is into this category that the poems of Rabindranath Tagore's *Gitanjali*
(Song Offerings) fall. Written in the early years of the twentieth century, and
translated from Bengali into English by the poet himself, these prose poems
(103 of them) are ways of saying goodbye to the material world in a language
that is certain of the eternal existence of the essential self. Here is the ninety-
fifth song:

I was not aware of the moment when I first crossed the threshold of
this life.
What was the power that made me open out into this vast mystery like
a bud in the forest at midnight!

When in the morning I looked upon the light I felt in a moment that I was no stranger in this world, that the inscrutable without name and form had taken me in its arms in the form of my mother.

Even so, in death the same unknown will appear as ever known to me. And because I love this life, I know I shall love death as well.

The child cries out when from the right breast the mother takes it away, in the very next moment to find in the left one its consolation.

Rabindranath Tagore, Gitanjali
(Branden Publishing Co., Boston, MA, USA, 1911)

You can see the connections between Tagore's lines and those of the *Bhagavad Gita* and the *Kena Upanishad*: the fascination with his place on the earth and a certainty that his own essence is indestructible. This concern with the continuity of the spirit and a strategy for becoming liberated from the cycle of death and rebirth is also present in a fascinating esoteric text called *The Tibetan Book of the Dead*, which offers guidance at the time of death and for the after-death state. It was translated into English in 1927 (but its origins as oral wisdom are unknown) and was immediately taken up by the psychoanalyst Carl Gustav Jung and other scholars, because it addresses itself to the big questions: Who am I? Why am I in this body? Where am I going? Why is there birth and why is there death?

These are some of the original questions posed in poetry, and we can see them running all through the centuries: in Alfred Lord Tennysson's 'In Memoriam', for example, which contains the wonderful verse that begins 'Be near me when my light is low' (this poem caused Queen Victoria to fall in love with his verse and Tennysson to be appointed poet laureate); in Rupert Brooke's 'If I should die, think only this of me'; in Dylan Thomas's villanelle for his dying father, 'Do Not Go Gentle Into That Goodnight'; and the Liverpool poet Roger McGough's 'Let Me Die a Young Man's Death'. And these are only some of the most popular.

The concern with the moment of death is present in the poetry of all ages and all cultures, as we shall see further when we come to look at Japanese haiku poetry.

WORDS OF POWER

But to return to *The Tibetan Book of the Dead*. This teaching contains mantras, which are words of power. When the devotee has learned them, they enable the devotee to 'close the womb-door' and so avoid the pain of another incarnation. It also contains some beautiful prayers for guidance while in the 'Bardo', which is the state between death and rebirth. In this state, it is held, the dead person sees visions which are entirely of their own making, so prayers may be sung to protect them from fear during this intermediary state. Here are a few lines from the prayers:

Abandoning all awe, fear and terror
May I recognize whatever appears as being my own thought-forms,
May I know them to be apparitions in the Intermediate State ...

When the bright radiances of the Five Wisdoms shine upon me now,
Let it come that I, neither awed nor terrified, may recognize
Them to be of myself ...

When the roarings of savage beasts are uttered,
Let it come that they be changed into the sacred sounds of
The Six Syllables;

When pursued by snow, rain, wind, and darkness,
Let it come that I see with the celestial eyes of bright Wisdom.

The six syllables referred to in this hymn are:

Om Mani Padme Hum
AUM MANI PAY ME HUNG

They are considered to be the essence of all happiness, prosperity and knowledge, and a great means of liberation. They mean 'the jewel is in the lotus': everything is exactly as it should be; there is no reason to fear, the whole universe is inside you so there is nothing to long for; and the universe is proceeding exactly as it should. No fear, only bliss.

When my elder daughter was little she loved to watch the He Man and She Ra cartoons. Although they appeared to me at first to be sexist superficial rubbish, when I watched them closely with her I saw that they were trying to capture a balance between the masculine and feminine forces (what Tibetan wisdom calls the 'yab-yum union', where the feminine stands for wisdom and the masculine for compassion) and explore ways of protecting the earth, our mother, from forces seeking to destroy her. The words He Man and She Ra became, in my daughter's four-year-old mind, her Syllables of Power, and she would run from room to room shouting them to herself while waving her arms around, returning to me finally in a state of exhilaration and contentment.

WHAT ARE YOUR OWN SIX WORDS OF POWER?

Go into your deep breathing again, close your eyes and sit quietly.

The first six words that come into your mind are your Power Words.

Consider them. Where do they come from?

Why have they assumed a potent quality?

What do they protect you against?

What do they lead you towards?

Write these words down on a piece of paper and simply play with them. Put them in any order you can imagine.

Write the word vertically down the page and then make another word, or phrase, out of every letter.

While you're doing this, chant them to yourself. Do you feel a rhythm emerging? Are they beginning to form themselves into phrases or sentences?

Observe the Mandelstam method, of just listening to hear what comes through the air to you.

When you feel that a poem is starting to take shape, write it down.

Concentrate on your breathing again as you look it over. Then, like the others, put it away.

This is the first draft of your third poem.

POWER AND POWERLESSNESS, AND THE POWER OF METAPHOR

The other side of power, where some of the ancients held that we could discover its greatest potency, is powerlessness. It is believed that the *Tao Te Ching* was probably written in the sixth century BCE by a sage called Lao Tsu. These exquisite poems were written down, so legend tells us, because a gatekeeper begged Lao Tsu, who was leaving town and riding off on his own into the desert because of what he saw as the decay of society, to commit to writing the heart of his teaching.

Although the title is notoriously hard to translate, Tao (pronounced Dow) can be understood as 'the way', Te (pronounced Deh) as 'virtue', and Ching as 'book'. The way and the virtue are themselves related, respectively, to the immense creative power of the universe and the ability of human beings to allow this power to flow through them.

The *Tao Te Ching* used the metaphor of water to explore the idea of this power that is also powerless; for example in Poem 8:

The highest good is like water.
Water gives life to the ten thousand things and does not strive.
It flows in places men reject and so is like the Tao ...

The 'ten thousand things' are everything that exists on the earth, including all our desires, distractions, phobias and hatreds. The poet uses the ten thousand things in order to write about states of being that are more abstract, more difficult to name or to make the reader experience. Here, Lao Tsu writes about water when he is trying to describe the highest good, because we all know what water is: we can see it, feel it, hear it, taste it and (sometimes) smell it. But we don't know the highest good. Water, one of the ten thousand things, is a way of beginning to understand it.

According to my reading of Lao Tsu, the heart of his teaching is about *not trying*, and it is this relaxed state I want you to cultivate in your poems. From Poem 16:

Empty yourself of everything.
Let the mind become still.
The ten thousand things will rise and fall while the Self
watches their return.
They grow and flourish and then return to the source.
Returning to the source is stillness, which is the way of nature.

Translated by Gia Fu Feng and Jane English (Vintage Books, New York, 1989)

What is an Image?

An 'Image' is that which presents an intellectual and emotional complex in an instant of time ... It is the presentation of such a 'complex' instantaneously which gives that sense of sudden liberation; that sense of freedom from time limits and space limits; that sense of sudden growth, which we experience in the presence of the greatest works of art.

It is better to present one Image in a lifetime that to produce voluminous works ...

Go in fear of abstractions. Do not retell in mediocre verse what has already been done in good prose ...

What the expert is tired of to-day the public will be tired of to-morrow ...

Don't be descriptive; remember that the painter can describe a landscape much better than you can and that he has to know a deal more about it.

When Shakespeare talks of the 'Dawn in russet mantle clad' he presents something which the painter does not present. There is little in this line that one can call description; he presents.

Consider the way of the scientists rather than the way of an advertising agent for a new soap.

The scientist does not expect to be acclaimed as a great scientist until he has discovered something. He begins by learning what has been discovered already. He goes from that point onward ... He does not expect his friends to applaud the results of his freshman classwork.

Ezra Pound, *The Literary Essays of Ezra Pound* (New Directions, USA, 1954)

I have discovered in my own writing that it is always a state of emptiness that enables the ten thousand things to rise and fall while the Self, the essential part of one's own self, watches their return. Poems never come to me when my mind is busy, only in moments of mind-enriching vacancy, where I have cleared my inner space (or it is accidentally cleared, say by gazing at the sea or the sky) so that the voices that want to be heard and the poems that want to come are allowed to move forward and make their presence felt.

You may object that the mind is (or only when in deepest sleep) never free of thoughts, and that you want to learn the craft of writing poems, not listen to some mumbo-jumbo about emptiness and returning to the source. Well, please believe me, this is indeed the craft. Ask any poet, any artist, and they will tell you that poems and art in general come from a mysterious place. You have, in silence, to allow yourself to be open to the mystery. If you concentrate on your breathing to take you into the stillness, and wait until the babble of your thoughts has quietened down, you will experience what is called 'the blue sky within', the spacious, open place from which you can watch the poems come to you.

The *Tao Te Ching* asks:

Who can wait quietly while the mud settles?
Who can remain still until the moment of action?

If you can learn to do these things, then your poems will become the poems they want to be.

ABSTRACT AND CONCRETE

I want you to turn now to some work on metaphor, which is the bridge between the ten thousand things and more abstract states that are sometimes hard to grasp. If any of your six Power Words are abstract, by which I mean words like 'Truth', 'Joy', 'Love' or 'Determination', words you can't actually form an image of in your mind, then write these down on another sheet of paper, as this exercise will enable you to explore them more completely. If not, simply choose two or three abstract nouns that resonate with you.

Now ask yourself 'What, in the material world, the world of the ten thousand things, does this word remind me of?' Give yourself half a page to explore each word, like this:

My word is ...

My word feels like ...

My words smells like ...

My word looks like ...

My word sounds like ...

My word tastes like ...

And what does my word do? How does it relax? How does it get through the night?

Add anything else that comes to mind about your word.

You will perhaps have noticed that I asked you to write similes at the beginning ('what is your word like?'), followed by metaphors. I think of similes as mirrors held up to reflect back the abstract word in a different way, and metaphors as lamps, where the abstraction is allowed to cast its mysterious light over the material world.

Here is a simile and a metaphor from Poem 77 of the *Tao Te Ching*:

The Tao of Heaven is like the bending of a bow.
The high is lowered, and the low is raised.
If the string is too long, it is shortened;
If there is not enough, it is made shorter.

The Tao of Heaven is to take from those who have too much
    and give to those who do not have enough.
Man's way is different.
He takes from those who do not have enough to give to those
    who already have too much.
What man has more than enough and gives it to the world?
Only the man of Tao.

It moves from the mysterious to the knowable world, from the Tao of Heaven to the wood and string of a bow, forming a bridge between the two different worlds. Indeed, the very word 'metaphor' comes from a Greek word which means 'to stretch over.'

Now make your own metaphors to bridge the two worlds. Do it now.

The metaphors you have written may not be poems in themselves, but as you continue to write you will find that metaphor is the driving force of your poems, their heart and foundation, their energy. There! The words I've just used are metaphors in themselves. A poem can't literally have a heart or a foundation, but metaphorically it can. And once you are aware of metaphor, you start to see how much it's used – not just in poems, but in newspapers, magazines, comics, films and paintings. One aspect of our humanness seems to be that we tend to describe things in terms of other things.

Why do you think this is? My own view is that we continually use metaphor because we feel an urgent need to make connections, make comparisons between different aspects of our world, and thereby find that it makes greater sense to us. We could almost say that everything is a metaphor for everything else, if we could just find the connection.

YOUR FIRST EPIC

We could also say that our major poems are the mirrors and lamps that we hold up in order to see ourselves – our behaviour, our ambitions, our loves, our tragedies – more clearly. This certainly seems to be true of *The Epic of Gilgamesh*, which has been described as 'the first great book of man's heart'.

Written on clay tablets around 2100BCE, *Gilgamesh* is, like all the ancient poems, far older, arising perhaps originally out of questions and wonder about our place in the universe. But it is different from the poems I've mentioned before, which explore how to achieve harmony between the human and the divine. *Gilgamesh* isn't like that. Its two main characters, King Gilgamesh and the wild man Enkidu, go about challenging the gods, kicking up a rumpus and being very annoying, until they are finally made to pay the price for their pride and rebellion. It's a mixture of an American buddy movie and Maurice Sendak's *Where the Wild Things Are*.

The story, briefly, goes like this. Gilgamesh is the King of Uruk (roughly equivalent to modern-day Iraq) and his people are fed up with him because of his tyranny, which includes demanding the first night with every bride before she has sex with her husband. They petition the gods to punish him, so the gods create a wild man, Enkidu, to fight and defeat the king. Enkidu is educated in sex and civilization by a sacred prostitute, so it seems hopeful that a more humane outcome will follow. But no ...

Enkidu and Gilgamesh fight through the streets of Uruk and the wild man finally gives in. Thus begins the first buddy movie: two men behaving badly, rampaging across heaven and earth, breaking divine decrees and generally overreaching themselves. They cut down the sacred cedar, defeat the Bull of Heaven, Taurus, and Gilgamesh refuses the advances of Ishtar, the goddess of sex and aggression, who should not be crossed lightly. Something has got to give.

So it's a poem about rebellion (why should the two men obey any laws at all?). But it is also about friendship, Gilgamesh and Enkidu putting themselves before everything else. And about finally having to accept that they will not live forever, they are not invulnerable.

The people appeal to the gods again, who decide that Enkidu will have to die. Gilgamesh laments his lost friend and tries to find a way to live forever himself. This involves crossing over into the land of the dead to meet Noah, who gives him a herb of rejuvenation which is (what filthy luck) stolen by a serpent when he gets back to the land of the living. So Gilgamesh finally has to prepare for death, as must we all at some time or other.

The poet Derek Hines has written his own version of this fabulous poem. Here is a short extract from near the end, when Gilgamesh is facing his own death:

So, to wait here,
swallowing this fist of fear in a quayside café
beside these old men
like rows of buttons waiting to be undone,
who rehearse their dignified farewells

against being snatched too quickly to say them;
trusting their shades will speak their goodbye
to those they love:

'Remember me as you saw me last
Gaming quietly with Spiro, my boyhood friend.
It was enough. I was ready when the Lady came.'

Lord now lettest thou ...

I am content at these warm zinc tables,
here among the click and slap-down
of backgammon counters,
like men unbuckling armour;

listening to the soft pencil-hatching of the evening's gossip
fill in the outline of what we've always known,
but will forget tonight
for the pleasure of hearing again tomorrow;

to sense, just under their tongues,
the ash of many ouzos –

Derek Hines, Gilgamesh *(Chatto and Windus, 2002)*

Did you notice the two similes in the extract? The old men 'like rows of buttons waiting to be undone,' and the sound of backgammon counters 'like men unbuckling armour'? The similes bring an enlargement to the bare narrative, giving us a sense of the feel and texture of the scene: old age like old clothes, and the memory of battle in the loud noises of the gaming-table.

Now, what would your own first epic be? You have written your first song and discovered your Words of Power, but what, for you, is the first great adventure? It may be an incident from your own life, or a tale you have heard or read in a newspaper, but let it be an event, or group of events, that you hold to be significant and somehow shaping. It doesn't have to be big, however. Eternity is in a grain of sand, and heaven in a wild flower, as William Blake wrote. An adventure can be the slightest thing: but it changes the world.

Spend some time breathing and relaxing, as you have before, and then write the first adventure that comes to your mind. The one that floats to the surface

What does a poem do? A poem evokes in the reader a poetic moment, close to that experienced by the poet. It can't be identical to that experienced by the poet because already the words will summon up aspects of the unique inner world of each person. Its spell conjures the reader away from the literal and conventional to the imaginative, from the purely mundane to the enchanted. In short, the poem is a means of re-enchanting a mostly dis-enchanted world. It opens up each person's inner cosmos where freedom is absolute apart from the contract with beauty, with the aesthetic. Prose invites judgments of social, political and rational truth. The poem whispers to you the ineffable, not social or political consensus. Because it's usually quite short, the memory of it can always be available to transform the moment, however oppressive the world outside. That's why poems are essential.

Judy Gahagan, Letters (unpublished)

first is the one that wants to be written now. Write it in free verse, simply beginning and ending your lines where it feels right. Don't try to make it rhyme, because rhyme can force your thoughts into shapes that aren't natural for them. (We'll explore rhyme later, and how you can harness its power without distorting your poems.) Try to write no more than forty lines. The chapter isn't ended yet and I don't want you exhausted before you've tried everything that is on offer.

HOWLING AT THE MOON

There must have been many moments in the lives of our ancestors, as indeed there are in our own, when tragedy strikes, everything conspires threateningly, and life feels very vulnerable. This state of affairs has produced, from ancient times to the present, some exquisitely heart-rending poetry. From the Book of Job in the Bible to our own modern poems of protest and rap, people have always suffered terrible pain and injustice, and the poets have, true to form, given voice to this pain.

We think that the Book of Job may have been committed to clay tablets around 500BCE, but of course it could be much older in its oral form. The story is told in prose at the beginning and end of the book, but the bulk of it, where Job laments his suffering and argues with those who come to talk with him, is poetry, reinforcing for us the fact that poetry was always the language of the most intense feelings and urgent thoughts.

Job is a good man with a large family. He farms, tends his animals, honours God and treats his neighbours well. He's done nothing wrong. The devil, however, who here is called 'the tester', asks God if he can probe Job's faith. God tells him to go ahead. So the tester takes everything away from Job: his lands, his family and his health. Job is left with absolutely nothing, and with suppurating skin to boot. Not pleasant. Friends of his come along and helpfully tell him that he must have done something wrong for which God is now punishing him. He hasn't, and he tells them so in no uncertain terms. Eventually he is so maddened by his so-called comforters and by his own pain that he's driven to this height of language:

2. How long will ye vex my soul, and break me to pieces with words?...
6. Know now that God hath overthrown me, and hath compassed me with his net.
7. Behold, I cry out of wrong, but I am not heard: I cry aloud, but there is no judgment.
8. He hath fenced up my way that I cannot pass, and he hath set darkness in my paths.
9. He hath stripped me of my glory, and taken the crown from my head.
10. He hath destroyed me on every side, and I am gone; and mine hope he hath removed like a tree ...
17. My breath is strange to my wife, though I intreated for the children's sake of mine own body...
20. My bone cleaveth to my skin and to my flesh, and I am escaped with the skin of my teeth.

The Book of Job, chapter 19 (King James Version)

This isn't the end of the story. Eventually, after some of the most beautiful poetry, Job has everything restored to him. But this is his wilderness time, his time for beating his breast and howling at the moon.

What is your own wilderness time? When you felt you had lost everything and were completely alone? When everyone seemed to have turned against you and you had no support? When the foundations of your whole life seemed to have collapsed? The nadir of your own life is a place from which very rich poetry can grow. It's fertilized with your bloody sweat, and watered with your tears, as the Garden of Gethsemane was before the Roman soldiers came to take Jesus away. So don't turn away from it, even though it might horrify you at first to look at it again.

Breathe. Go into this dark place. Don't flinch. Look at it. Hear its sounds, taste its tastes, breathe in its smells. Feel it again. Now simply write it down in terms of all its sense-impressions. In prose if you like, if that will help you to write it more flowingly. Afterwards, you may want to break it up into shorter lines. But for now, write without stopping. Just write.

With this one in particular, put it away as soon as you've written it. I'd like you to get some distance from it immediately (and I don't want you tearing it up!) so that when you come back to it you can look at it coolly, almost as an outsider would, to see what works and what doesn't.

You may sometimes find that you want to tear up one of your poems. Don't. I can't emphasize this strongly enough. Even if it is, in total, a failure, there will always be a line or a phrase or even just one word that you can use in another poem. Poets recycle all the time. And you may find, later, that it's not a failure at all. You might send it to a magazine or a poetry competition and be very surprised to discover that an editor or a judge likes it. There's no accounting for taste, not even your own.

The Riddles of the Sphinx

The world is a mysterious place, perhaps just as hard for us to understand as it was for our ancestors. One of the things they invented, to help them enjoy life's mystery, was riddles. Instead of trying to make things clear, they made them more opaque, more difficult to grasp. They posed conundrums to one another in the spirit of play, perhaps to make the mysteries less threatening, or perhaps because they simply enjoyed them. Sometimes it can be pleasurable not to understand something, and to struggle with it until it finally reveals itself. They are also known as kennings ('knowings') from which we get the words 'cunning' and 'con man', and they're particularly useful for your writing because they show you how to get your tongue around an object and get to know it from the inside.

Riddles enable the reader to reach into the heart of the subject being described, described as it is from the inside, from its own secret self, so we begin to get a sense of how it thinks and feels. Riddles are living metaphors, because the object is described as itself, but mysteriously, as though it were other than itself.

Writing riddles is therefore a tremendously vivifying act for a poet. They make you, and your reader, see something in a new and somehow shivery sort of way. They make the known world unknown, and then they make it known again. They wake the world up, out of its familiar sleepy patterns. And this is, at heart, one of the main tasks of poetry.

Try three riddles of your own now. I would like you to take, one by one, three objects that are ordinary, familiar, even hardly noticeable to you. Things you have around you every day. Now, one by one, using your breathing and your dreaming relaxation, step into the object. Feel what it is like to be this thing. Feel what it is like to be held, to be used, to be put aside. Feel what it is like to hang around, if that is what the object does, or to have something standing upon you. Let yourself become other than you are and be these three objects.

When the sphinx asked Oedipus her famous riddle ('What walks on four legs in the morning, two legs at noon and three in the evening?') she was enquiring into what it means to be a man. Because it is a man who crawls on four legs in the morning of his life, walks on two as an able-bodied adult, and on three when he walks with the help of a stick as his sun begins to sink. Riddles ask us what it means to be in this world of ten thousand things. They enable us to discover the world again and again, to remind ourselves of its mystery by allowing ourselves to experience the inner life of objects other than ourselves, and begin to understand our kinship with them.

REVIEWING YOUR WORK

Now comes the fun part, where you look at everything you have achieved while you have been working on this chapter.

Take all the poems out of their box or drawer and lie them on the floor.

Read them through carefully, one by one. In doing this, you will get a sense of what are your deepest concerns. You will find out more about where your need to write poems comes from. You may not have been conscious of this when you were doing the writing, but it will begin to reveal itself to you now.

Once you have done this, there are two things I want you to look at in these first poems: your vowels and your metaphors.

Do your vowels carry the feeling you want your words to convey? Underline any that don't last as long as they should, or move too slowly, and find others that give the poem the rhythm it wants to have. Say the poems out loud to yourself so you can hear how fast or how slowly they move. Walk around the room to the rhythm of your poems; stamp them out, as our ancestors would have. If a vowel is dragging your poem back, adjust it. If a vowel is pulling you forwards too quickly, change that too.

The question I want you to ask of your metaphors is: do they feel natural? Do they seem to arise easily out of the world of ten thousand things and then sink back into the abstraction you want to illuminate?

Your aim, in your metaphors, is to create a sense of surprise and inevitability at the same time. A tall order I know, but test them out on your body. If they make you tremble inside, but leave you with a sense of ease, as if they are right, then they are right. If they leave you uneasy, a little irritated, then the abstraction and the concrete image you have brought in to illuminate it don't quite fit together. You may be almost there, so let it sit in your mind for a spell. The new image will come to you, probably when you are doing something quite else and not thinking about metaphor at all. All very inconvenient, as poetry generally is.

And after all this, it's time for a rest. You need to give yourself a good breathing space between each spate of work, because this is when the poems hibernate inside you and sometimes a new poem will gestate. Once you have started along this road, you keep going, whether you know it or not. So allow yourself a week's rest and recuperation. But stay alert. A poem might creep up on you just when you are least expecting one.

2 Nature Poems

Earth. We all come from it and we all go back to it. Earth to earth.

Do you remember your early wonders about where you came from? In the front garden of our council house I stood by the yellow Rose of Sharon bush, contemplating my father's words when I had asked him the question. Some seeds grow into flowers, and some seeds grow into babies, he told me. My infant mind was delighted at the different possibilities, and I scoured the lawn, the concrete path, clover, little dorrit, and those bright indigo flowers whose name I forget, trying to predict which seed might become a human child. Like the ancients, I was in awe of the mystery of growth, the rings of a cut tree signifying years, the sudden appearance of crocuses, the tremendous return of spring, just when I wasn't expecting it.

Ted Hughes called the snowdrop 'implacable'; Gerard Manley Hopkins said that nature is 'never spent', and T.S. Eliot wrote of 'lilacs out of the dead land'. Nature is so rich that we cannot fathom her, cannot get her measure. She keeps coming back, it seems, no matter what we do to her, and no matter how much harm we do. Here in London we seem to have run out of sparrows, apparently because of the new lead-free petrol. So what do we have now, in our little garden in Stepney? More magpies, blackbirds, squirrels and frogs. Nature doesn't seem to mind that one species disappears for a while. There are plenty more, pushing and shoving, making the garden come alive with their calls and their scurryings.

Ted Hughes paid tribute to the earth's tremendous talent for returning in his poem 'March morning unlike others'. In it, he describes one of the first days of spring, when the snows and rains have gone. There is, for the first time in the year, 'Leisure to stand' and lambs are 'freed to be foolish'. He describes the earth as a gigantic patient 'invalid, dropsied, bruised, wheeled / Out into the sun, / After the frightful operation.' Isn't that a lovely metaphor? Winter is likened to a frightful operation: which it is. We feel we are being cut open in the darkest part of the year. We want to hibernate, but we still have to rise in the cold darkness and go out to work – *cut*. We are ill with unnameable viruses – *cut, cut*. We see the ground and the trees monochrome, bare of any comfort or colour – *cut, cut, cut*. By March we are so ragged that we hardly know who we are. Then we look at the ground, even at the cracks between pavement slabs, and we see that a secret husbandry has been taking place. Bright green shoots are pushing up.

> She lies back, wounds undressed to the sun,
> To be healed,
> Sheltered from the sneapy chill creeping North wind,
> Leans back, eyes closed, exhausted, smiling
> Into the sun.

Look at the way Hughes slows us down, here, to enable us to enjoy the moment: 'She lies back ... / To be healed ... Leans back ... Into the sun.' One way to slow the reader down is to put two stressed syllables together: lies back, leans back. We have to say them slowly in our heads, so we are forced to step back and survey the scene. These two stressed syllables together are called a 'spondee'. You will find one whenever a poet wants to draw your attention to something wonderful.

You see this slowing down, too, in Gerard Manley Hopkins' poem 'Pied Beauty'. Written in 1877 and never published during the poet's lifetime, it can still stop your heart with the concentration of its adoration and praise:

> Glory be to God for dappled things –
> For skies of couple-colour as a brinded cow;
> For rose-moles all in stipple upon trout that swim;
> Fresh firecoal chestnut-falls, finches' wings;
> Landscape plotted and pieced – fold, fallow and plough;
> And áll trádes, their gear and tackle and trim.
>
> All things counter, original, spare, strange;
> Whatever is fickle, freckled (who knows how?)
> With swift-slow; sweet, sour; adazzle, dim;
> He fathers-forth whose beauty is past change:
> Praise him.

Hopkins believed that every word contained its own inner landscape, that each word was a world in itself, and that the poet's job is to help the reader to discover that inner world. One of the ways he tried to do this was by the use of what he called 'sprung rhythm', which is the rhythms of everyday speech, irregular and unpredictable. You can see the sudden spondees erupting here in 'all trades', which he has stressed to bring you up short even more; in the list of adjectives near the end: 'swift-slow; sweet, sour; adazzle, dim;' which cause you to think more deeply about the nature of freckledness – and in the final 'Praise him' which ends the poem in a glorious shout of praise.

I think you may well have felt this sudden wonder at a shoot of green, for example, when you thought that everything was dead. Or at bright pink camellia buds bursting over a wall when you stepped outside on a bitter

February morning. Today I walked to Tower Bridge down Cable Street, all concrete, but when I reached the bus-stop the trampled ground all around it was alive with yellow crocuses: what the poet and novelist Michèle Roberts has called 'an insurrection of crocuses', as if the spring were in mighty rebellion against the old regime of winter.

What can you do in the face of such miracles? The poet Rainer Maria Rilke suggested that there is only one response: praise. And praise is one of poetry's great aspects. Whether or not you believe in any divine creative force, something miraculous is definitely happening. How could something so beautiful not be miraculous?

VENTURING OUTSIDE

One of the poet's tasks is to bear witness to these changes and upheavals that take place within and upon the body of the earth. So put on some suitable clothes, put your notebook and your pen in your pocket – and this book too – and leave the place where you live. Lock the door behind you, take a deep breath and start walking. It doesn't matter where you go, because Nature is everywhere. You'll find her on the densest housing estate or industrial area, in car parks, building sites and waste land. Especially waste land.

THE IAMBIC FOOT

I want you to be aware of your feet as they move along the ground, and the movement of your body as you find your rhythm. If you are using sticks or crutches, your rhythm might be different again. Feel it, count it out, one two, one two, a marching rhythm or a limping rhythm, the most popular and natural-sounding measure in the language.

It's called the 'iambic foot'. The ancient Greeks, from whom we have inherited our understanding of metre, measured everything in feet, probably because they danced and sang their poems. But whereas the Greeks measured long and short syllables, we have hard syllables and soft syllables, or strong ones and weak ones, depending on how you like to think of them. This is because of the influence of the northern European tribes, who invaded us after the Romans left, and gave us strong alliterative poetry, where it didn't matter how many syllables there were in a line as long as there were the right number of stresses (four), and that the important words began with the same consonant. It was the energy of this Anglo-Saxon poetry that Gerard Manley Hopkins was trying to recapture in his own ecstatic alliterative poetry, written during Queen Victoria's reign over a thousand years later.

Let's stay with the iambic foot for now, though, and the iambic line beloved by Chaucer, Shakespeare, Sir Thomas Wyatt – it would be tedious to continue the list, because it has been used by so many poets: it feels so natural, so close to the rhythms of our everyday speech. Count it out as you walk along: 'di dum, di dum, di dum, di dum, di dum ...'. Five iambs in a line is called an 'iambic pentameter'. That is the metre of all sonnets and of all of Shakespeare's plays.

But it is not compulsory to have five. If you have one iamb in a line, it is called an iambic 'monometer'. Two would be an iambic 'dimeter', three a 'trimeter', four a 'tetrameter', six a 'hexameter', seven a 'septameter', eight an 'octameter', nine a 'nonameter' – and I can't remember ten, but you will probably never want to write a line that long anyway. Although, then again, perhaps you will!

The iamb means 'a lame man' and when I have shown you some poems in this metre you will see how they move slowly, determinedly, along. Take a look at this verse from William Wordsworth's poem 'To A Butterfly' (probably written around 1800):

This plot of orchard-ground is ours;
My trees they are, my Sister's flowers;
Here rest your wings when they are weary;
Here lodge as in a sanctuary!
Come often to us, fear no wrong;
Sit near us on the bough!
We'll talk of sunshine and of song,
And summer days, when we were young;
Sweet childish days, that were as long
As twenty days are now.

and this, from a 'Tracking Poem', by the American poet Adrienne Rich, published in 1986:

The tobacco fields lie fallow   the migrant pickers
no longer visible
where undocumented intelligences travailed
on earth they had no stake in
though the dark leaves growing beneath white veils
were beautiful   and the barns opened out like fans
All this of course could have been done differently
This valley itself: one more contradiction
the paradise fields   the brute skyscrapers
the pesticidal wells

The Fact of a Doorframe – Selected Poems 1950–2001
(*W W Norton & Co Inc, 2002*)

They are two very different poems, but you can feel the iambic foot plodding through both of them, Not all the time of course. That would be boring, and send the reader to sleep. If you mark the strong beats and the weak beats, you will see how the poets have varied their metre when they wanted to change the pace or the mood of the poem. But the iambic foot holds them together.

Let the iamb do this work for your own poem now. You have been walking for a while, so sit down on a bench, on a wall, or lean against a railing if there's no seat. Cast your eyes around. What's the first thing you see that's growing? Look hard at it. When you're ready, go up close. Feel it. Smell it. Listen for any sounds it makes. Now sit down again and get out your notebook and pen. Let the iambic metre walk slowly through your body, slowing down your breath and your thoughts. Now begin to describe this growing thing in your notebook. Don't try consciously to impose the iambic metre on your language. That will happen naturally, from the rhythm of your walking. And when the rhythm doesn't want to be iambic, because of some rush of energy in the poem, or when the poem needs to slow right down, that will happen of its own accord too. Remember that you are not the source of the poem: it is simply flowing through you. Your job is to allow yourself to become as hollow as a reed or a stick of bamboo so the words can flow as they want to.

Let as many lines come as you can. Iambic lines tend to open out and come to their point in their own time, so don't rush yourself or think that the poem's finished after only eight lines: it might well not be. And when you are sure you have finished this first draft, sit a bit longer. Let the poem sink into your body, become part of you. Say it out loud in the air (no one will notice: everyone talks to themselves nowadays) so you can hear the beat. Tap the beat with your feet. Can you hear the pilgrim movement of your thoughts as they search for the right word, the expression or metaphor that will offer this growing thing to the reader in a language that will make them feel they are there with you, experiencing it, taking it in?

HAIKU, TANKA AND RENGA

If you can, stay outside, and get walking again. We'll move away from metre for a while now, so you don't become hypnotized by the iambic foot, and do some work on three Japanese verse forms that may be the most concentrated kinds of written expression we have. They don't count stresses, they only count syllables, so they will be a change from the metre you've had inside your body up to now today.

One of the great practitioners of haiku was Matsuo Basho (not his real name – he called himself after his favourite banana tree) who was writing in the seventeenth century. So when England was having its great plague and great fire, and was caught up in its Civil War, Basho was wandering all over Japan practicing *sabi* (contented solitude), *wabi* (the spirit of poverty) and learning to merge himself with the objects of his vision so that, through his haiku, he could become what he was looking at. You could say that haiku are the strongest kind of metaphor, because in them the poet stretches over and enters into the essence of the object he is observing.

Here are some of my favourite Basho haiku:

Samurai talking –
Now I taste the salty tang
Of fresh horseradish

How happy I am
Only this once not to see
Mount Fuji through mist

When the fire burns high
In my mind it's becoming
a sizzling snowball!

You the butterfly
And I the deep dreaming heart
Of Emperor Chuang Tsu.

In 'Samurai talk' can you get the sense of how warriors, or any strong men, often smell strong? Not bad, but strong – like horseradish? If you've ever pulled up some horseradish and eaten it straight out of the ground, you will know what I mean. It hits the back of your mouth and makes you think you're going to fall over. Basho is drawing together a sound, the Samurai talking together, a taste and a smell, the tang of horseradish (isn't tang a good word?) and making us feel the connections between the two.

Can you sense the strange ambiguity in the Mount Fuji haiku? I always wonder whether he means he's glad that the mist isn't shrouding the mountain today, or glad that the mist is so thick that he can't see Fuji at all. That's what haiku does, too: takes us into the mystery of the object and the ambiguity of the poet's relationship with it.

You can see this mystery most clearly in the butterfly haiku. It is based on a dream that the Emperor Chuang Tsu had, that he was a butterfly. After his dream, he didn't know whether he was an emperor dreaming he was a butterfly, or a butterfly dreaming he was an emperor. And Basho has used this image to write a love poem, where the lover has merged so far into his beloved that the boundaries are utterly lost.

It is this merging with the object that I want you to work on now. Keep walking until you see something that catches your attention, then attend to it. Then do more than that: move into it, feel that you've become it. Dream yourself into it until your own life and the object's life seem to be intertwined.

The Japanese word that heralds this merging is *kireji*. By this they mean a cutting word that takes the poem from the description of an object into an illumination of it: the object suddenly experienced from the inside or from some unlooked-for, unpredictable angle. So in 'Light the fire', we are looking at a fire and then, after a dash (which is often the English equivalent of the cutting word) we are forced to contemplate a giant snowball. Why? Well, do you remember coming in from the cold, your hands freezing, and then they suddenly start to feel very hot? Do you feel that cold and hot seem to go together? And have you seen that sometimes a fire can be so hot that its heart will look like snow?

In your own haiku, allow yourself to make these strange connections. Haiku don't have to make logical sense. They are written in order to draw attention to the deepest connections between things, the connections we don't easily make with our conscious minds. Every one is a minor miracle.

Now let's look at the technique of how to write them. The rules of haiku writing are strict and rarely broken. The first line should have five syllables, the second seven and the third five. That's all. Sounds impossible, doesn't it? But Basho believed that the more intense the emotion, the fewer syllables were required, and that if the feeling was especially intense, even seventeen syllables could be too many. Here, however, we'll stick to seventeen.

As you look at your object and the words begin to come, count out their syllables on your fingers. Before you write your poem down, compose it out loud in the air, as a mantra, as syllables of power. You'll notice that the counting of syllables makes the words recede into the background, and this is quite a lovely experience: the magic of numbers dancing with the magic of words.

Write it down.

Now walk twenty more paces and find something else to merge with. And do the whole thing all over again.

Haiku is a wonderful practice. Writing haiku trains you in finding the essence of things, in metaphor, in making connections that you didn't know were there. So it is worth giving yourself some time on them, say a week. Try going out each day and waylaying two objects. Fourteen haiku in seven days. And don't think 'Steady on! That's going it a bit', because the whole aim of haiku is to compose fast, to step into something and then move on. Its inspiration derives partly from Zen Buddhism, where the present moment is all that counts. In the poet William Blake's words, you are aiming to kiss a joy as it flies, rather than pinning anything down. That would kill it, and a haiku is a living thing.

You may find, after the initial exhilaration of making haiku, that seventeen syllables is constricting. If you want to write more, then you can try the earlier verse form called the 'tanka'. This consists of a haiku, then a line space, then a 'wakuru', which means 'accompanying verse', and consists of two lines of seven syllables each. A tanka will enable you to explore your moment of illumination further, or perhaps build up to it more slowly. And if you've fallen in love with syllabic verse, counting syllables quietly on your fingers all the time, try the 'renga' (braided verse), which goes haiku – wakuru – haiku – wakuru – haiku – wakuru, for as long as you want. In a renga, you might tell the story of a tree over a whole year, or narrate the changes in your relationship with a magpie, or a crow.

Here's one I made earlier.

Sparrow Trying to Catch a Feather: A Renga

Outside my window
a seagull's breast feather, small,
curved and white, but full

as it curves, essence of curved
breast within itself, floats up

and down on curving
air, and a sparrow, perhaps
building its nest, is

trying to catch it in its beak.
The feather rises and falls –

mischievously? – and
the sparrow rises and falls
too. But the sparrow

is heavier than the feather,
and his little black face bobs

up and down, feather
always slightly ahead. I
know that birds with their

lovely hollow bones defy
gravity, but this one is

bouncing on little
wings through the air, which lifts the
feather always just

beyond him, so he has to
defy it just that bit more –

all for his nest? Is
it the urgency to make
a home that has him

bobbing up and down in the
air with such a determined

expression? Perhaps

not, because when the feather
lands on the pitched roof

nearby – here, take me, part of
another bird's body, for

your own nest – he's lost
interest. I think it was
just joy had him in

the air rising and tumbling
just beyond my window, the

knowledge that, though things
tend to fall, he and his prey
were up in the air

of the morning, each in their
own presence, rising, floating,

against the calling
importunity of the
seagulls on the roofs,

the schoolchildren with their songs,
that occupy the playground.

Julia Casterton

There is yet another form, a mixture of haiku and prose, called the 'haibun', where the Japanese poets kept a record of their journeys. Sometimes they travelled together, sometimes alone, meeting up at a sacred shrine or a priest-poet's house to compose haiku together. Their journeys over the mountains were often dangerous, but they would need no protection from any human being because they possessed nothing of any material value. Their writing and painting were their treasures, and, as these were some of the high arts (along with the tea ceremony, flower-arranging and making gardens), the poets were well-revered, and given rice and greens by householders when they were hungry.

Here's a short extract from Basho's *Narrow Road to the Deep North*, the account of his final journey, on the course of which he died:

Turning away from the highroad leading to the provinces of Nambu, I came to the village of Iwate, where I stopped overnight. The next day, I looked at the cape of Oguru and the tiny island of Mizu, both in a river, and arrived by way of Naruko hot spring at the barrier-gate of Shitomae which blocked the entrance to the province of Dewa. The gate-keepers were extremely suspicious, for very few travellers dared to pass this difficult road under normal circumstances. I was admitted after long waiting, so that darkness overtook me while I was climbing a huge mountain. I put up at a gate-keeper's house which I was very lucky to find in such a lonely place. A storm came upon us and I was held up for three days.

Bitten by fleas and lice,
I slept in a bed,
A horse urinating all the time
Close to my pillow

According to the gate-keeper, there was a huge body of mountains obstructing my way to the province of Dewa, and the road was terribly uncertain. So I decided to hire a guide. The gate-keeper was kind enough to find me a young man of tremendous physique, who walked in front of me with a carved sword strapped at his waist and a stick of oak gripped firmly in his hand. I myself followed him, afraid of what might happen on the way. What the gate-keeper had told me turned out to be true. The mountains were so thickly covered with foliage and the air was so hushed that I felt as if I were groping my way in the dead of night. There was not even the cry of a single bird to be heard, and the wind seemed to breathe out black soot through every rift in the hanging clouds.

Matsuo Basho, The Narrow Road to the Deep North, *and other*
Travel Sketches *(Translated by Nobuyuki Yuasa)*
(Penguin Books, 1966), pp. 120–121

Bear in mind, when you try your own haibun, that the tradition established by the early masters involved turning away from nothing: the fleas, the horse's urine, the danger of the journey. In other places we find the sadness of concubines and detailed descriptions of physical ailments such as dysentery. The pleasure of reading haibun emerges partly from the fact that they are as far away as possible from the kind of travel writing that only tells the glamorous things about travel. Because moving around can be hard. We do it because it makes us feel intensely alive (the poet W.B. Yeats said 'old men should be explorers') and changes our experience of home when we return.

One of the aims of Zen Buddhism is to be conscious at all times, even at the moment of death. Basho's final haiku can be translated something like this:

When I was on my journey
Old by now and very ill
Dreams still wandered on

which gives the sense of consciousness persisting, even though the physical body can no longer continue.

Now let's try a shortened version of Basho's enormous journey, one the poet Judy Gahagan has called 'one hundred metre tourism', and which you can complete in a single afternoon. As long travel involves huge logistical arrangements which take up your thoughts and steal your leisure, a short trip can give you the freedom to write without having to worry about planes, passports or suitcases. All you need is a bottle of water in case you get thirsty.

Choose a place not too far away that you have always wanted to visit. It may be a house, a wood, a park, a church or a football ground: somewhere you've not been before. Now just walk there at half the pace you normally walk, taking in as much as you can as you go, and stopping at intervals to write down your observations. The aim is to see familiar territory as a foreign land. By moving slowly through places you know, you see them with fresh, more innocent eyes, the eyes of a wanderer or a seeker. At first you might think 'Oh no, this is so boring' but you'll find that even very familiar roads look different when you're not hurrying through them.

In your everyday life, you rush around in order to make things happen: travelling to work, shopping, going to meet a friend. But, as W.H. Auden said, poetry makes nothing happen – in the outer world. Instead, it brings all happenings inside itself and creates a silence around them so they can be appreciated in a new way. It offers us the most ordinary things as if they were new-found, as if they were miracles – which they are. It's a wonder anything exists at all considering the threat we've placed it under.

When your eyes catch something that arrests them, stop. Think of your prose narrative as walking and your haiku as stopping. The haiku is for when you've been slowed down by the sight of something. Write your haiku (5–7–5 syllables with a cutting word or dash, remember) and then move on, stopping again after a little while to continue your observations in prose.

And after your short journey, read through all your haiku, tanka, renga and haibun, before putting them away in your Nature folder.

THE PILGRIMAGE

I now want you to try a longer journey, a pilgrimage to a sacred site, or to a place that is important to you. It doesn't matter if you have no sense of the sacred, because, if Hindu theology is anything to go by, any place you love will be your church. If you're unable to travel, you can use your memory and your imagination, going over in your mind a location of special energy or beauty. For this poem we're going to try a variation of the 'terza rima', the form Dante invented for *The Divine Comedy*, which begins in a dark wood, has him travelling with the poet Virgil into Hell and Purgatory, and then following Beatrice, his beloved, into Paradise.

Terza rima simply means 'third rhyme'. It consists of as many three line stanzas as you want. You might be interested to note that the word 'stanza' means 'room'. The Italians called them that. You can picture your reader going from one room to the next in your poem. The earlier Latin word is 'vers' which means 'a furrow'. You follow the plough down one furrow and follow it back down another. Two ways of thinking about the way we divide poetry up.

In *The Divine Comedy* the rhyme goes:

A the first line rhyming with
B the third and the second hooking
A over into the next stanza to

B become the first and third of
C that one. The second line always
B reaches over into the following

C stanza, creating a kind of
D back-stitch effect, where every
C stanza seems to look both

D forwards and back.
E
D

And here are the opening stanzas of *The Divine Comedy*, so you can see how the rhymes work in Italian:

Nel mezzo del cammin di nostra vita
mi ritrovai per una selva oscura
che la diritta via era smarrita.
Ah quanto a dir qual era e cosa dura
esta selva selvaggia e aspra e forte
che nel pensier rinova la paura!
Tant' e amara che poco e piu morte;
ma per trattar den ben ch'io vi trovai,
diro dell'arte cose ch'i' v'ho scorte.
Io no so ben ridir com' io v'entrai,
tant'era pieno di sonno a quel punto
che la verace via abbandonai.

(In the middle of the journey of our life I came to myself within a dark wood where the straight way was lost. Ah, how hard a thing it is to tell of that wood, savage and harsh and dense, the thought of which renews my fear! So bitter is it that death is hardly more. But to give account of the good which I found there I will tell of the other things I noted there.

I cannot rightly tell how I entered there, I was so full of sleep at that moment when I left the true way...)

> *Dante, Italian text with translation and commentary by John D. Sinclair*
> *(Oxford University Press, 1939)*

But the problem with terza rima is that it doesn't translate so easily from Italian to English, because whereas in Italian many words end in vowel sounds, making it easy to rhyme without sounding forced, in English many of our words are so definite that the rhyme can sound over-emphatic. And there are few things worse than pushy rhymes: they can shove the whole feeling and meaning of the poem off in the wrong direction.

What T.S. Eliot suggested as a solution to this problem (a solution he used himself in a part of his third Quartet, 'Little Gidding') was to use alternate masculine and feminine endings instead of rhyme. And what, you may ask, are masculine and feminine endings? Well, a masculine ending has a stressed syllable at the end of the line, like this:

Here we are again

and a feminine ending an unstressed one:

in the long-house.

Using each ending on alternate lines gives a kind of ghost rhyme, a feeling of similarity without the certainty of rhyme.

Seamus Heaney used a mixture of rhyme and alternate masculine and feminine endings in his narrative sequence *Station Island*, published in 1984. Station Island is a site of pilgrimage on Lough Derg in County Donegal, and the poem itself is a series of dream encounters with people from the poet's life, presences evoked through the silence and the fasting of a pilgrimage, which here involves walking barefoot and praying round the 'beds', which are stone circles believed to be the remains of early medieval monastic cells.

Here is something from the seventh section of the poem, where the narrator becomes aware of the presence of a man he knew who has been murdered in sectarian violence:

Through life and death he had hardly aged.
There always was an athlete's cleanliness
shining off him and except for the ravaged

forehead and the blood, he was still the same
rangy midfielder in a blue jersey
and stretched pants, the one stylist on the team,

the perfect, clean, unthinkable victim.
'Forgive the way I have lived indifferent –
forgive my timid circumspect involvement,'

I surprised myself by saying. 'Forgive
my eye,' he said, 'all that's above my head.'
And then a stun of pain seemed to go through him

and he trembled like a heatwave and faded.

Earth. We all come from it and we all go back to it. By making contact with the earth, the poet is able to speak with a man who has been untimely killed and returned there. By making his pilgrimage and looking at the water, he is able to sense 'a presence/entering into my concentration' and speak with the man's spirit in a way that would not have been possible had he not been involved in the committed awareness that a pilgrimage requires and exacts.

Think now where you would like to go – to a cathedral or a wood, on foot or on the bus, by land or by sea – and start to picture the place so you imagine what it's like before you get there. Write down, in note-form, your expectations of what it will look like, sound like, feel like, smell like and taste like. The essence of the place is inside you already: your task now is to give it a body for your reader by going there and experiencing it in all its literal detail.

Perhaps in ancient times every walk was a pilgrimage. There is a theory that ley lines, lines of energy and power that criss-cross all countries, were once simply the quickest route between different places, signposted by ponds, hills and stones, hallowed and charged over millennia by the walking of countless feet. In the film *Seven Years in Tibet*, about an Austrian climber's relationship with the young Dalai Lama, we see the Tibetans walking, walking endlessly over their holy land, walking with the awareness that, as Gerard Manley Hopkins put it 'The earth is charged with the grandeur of God.' It is this charged quality that I want you to concentrate on, so that you can catch the bursting nature, the fullness of the experience of being a pilgrim, a word whose meaning has to do with being a stranger in a strange land, taken in the first place, it's thought, from the practice of falconry, where the peregrine falcons were caught, not in the nest, but while they were in flight. Your pilgrimage poems will be you yourself, as you catch yourself in flight.

But first look down and consider your feet. These are what you go on, and the going can be very hard. On your feet, as on your hands, is written the whole history of your life, because if your hands form your point of interaction with the world through objects and people, the things you touch, then your feet connect you with everything that ever grew and everyone who was ever buried, through their constant walking on the earth. If the earth is our mother, then it is through our feet that we keep in contact with her.

Here's part of a poem called 'Feet' by Denise Levertov (who was born in England, but lived most of her adult life in North America), from her posthumous collection *This Great Unknowing* (New Directions, 1999).

We begin our lives with such small,
   such plump and perfect
      infant feet, slivers of pink pearl for toenails,
it's laughable to think of their ever sustaining
   the whole weight of a body.
      And end them sometimes
with gnarled and twisted objects
   in which are inscribed
      whole histories – wars, and uprootings,
and long
   patient or impatient sufferings,
      layer beyond layer,
successions of light and shadow, whole ranges.
   But no recollection
      of what our feet were like
before we put them to work.

I often spend time in Galicia, in a small fishing village called Finisterre, which is where pilgrims arrive for some sun-worship after their thousand kilometre-long pilgrimage to the shrine of Saint James in Santiago de Compostella. As they sit exhausted in one of the little cafes overlooking the harbour, they take off their sandals and gaze in utter astonishment at their feet. These little things have brought them this far! I want you to give your feet the silent wonder treatment before you go on your pilgrimage. What do they tell you about what you've walked through already?

Take your shoes off and wash your feet in a bowl of warm water. As you soap them, massage them with a strong but gentle touch all over: on the soles and heels, the instep, the balls of the toes and between the toes, and on the 'webbing' which hold the toes together. Massage the bones on the top of the foot and the tendons down either side. In Eastern thought, this opens up the chakras (or wheels of energy) underneath your feet to enable you to gain more strength from the earth as you walk along. Whether or not you believe that, it will certainly make your feet feel more alive before you begin.

Now dry your feet and look at them on the towel. Your pilgrimage is going to take you somewhere new that you've long wanted to visit, somewhere familiar that you've long wished to return to, or perhaps to a person you admire and want to talk with and listen to. But where have your feet taken you up to now? On your feet, as on your hands, you can see the marks, scars and bumps that reveal what you've done, the life you've already lived, the shoes you've worn, the terrain you've crossed. As you look at your feet, let them take you into a reverie about your past journeys, your past flights and returns. What do these journeys tell you about your love of exploration and your feelings about returning home? If our whole self is inscribed in our body, its ease and disease, its tensions and relaxations, its roughnesses and smoothnesses, then the feet can be used as a wonderful way into the story.

Your feet are your first station, your first standing place. As you begin your poem, think of all the places they have walked before and allow the iambic foot to enter again into your body, so you can feel the walking rhythm even before you start to walk. Write roughly ten syllables in each line and aim for alternate masculine and feminine endings. Make this first poem about ten stanzas long, with three lines in every stanza. Take the reader from room to room in your thoughts as you tour the house of your life.

Now begin your pilgrimage. However long you intend to be away, be vigilant, now, for the arrival of your next station, your next standing-place. As with the haiku, this will be when something or someone (a stone, a person, an animal) arrests your attention and you feel bound to wait until you have taken it in and let it enter your poem. Each station is a site of listening and looking, where all your senses are alert and you are ready to allow a new experience in.

As you observe, listen to and feel the experience, reflect on how it changes you. If character is destiny, then the fact that you have decided to go on a pilgrimage will also affect your character, the way you see the world. The dead man who appeared to Seamus Heaney in *Station Island* caused him to reconsider his commitment to his neighbours and his community, and to ask forgiveness of the ghost for his own indifference.

Travelling along, you have ample time to reflect upon the way-stations of your past, the places and people who have caused you to stay in one place for a while. As they come to you, honour them in your poem, and consider the effects they had in your life, and you in theirs. Your station can occur as the result of a memory just as easily as of an encounter in the outside world. Think of them as meeting-places, but remember that the meeting can take place in your mind. As the mind is rarely still, but makes connections all the time between what's happening in the present and what's gone before or is yet to come, you will find that people and events from your past present themselves to you on your pilgrimage, as do your projections about your future.

Don't ignore anything. Do you feel uncomfortable in your body? There's a station. Stop and attend to it. It may be the first poem you write on your way.

Here's part of Robert Burns' 'Address to the Tooth-Ache' (written by the author at a time when he was grievously tormented by that disorder):

My curse on your envenomed stang
That shoots my tortured gums alang,
An' thro' my lugs gies mony a bang
　　Wi' gnawin vengeance;
Tearin' my nerves wi' bitter twang,
　　Like racking engines ...

Whare'er that place be, priests ca' hell,
Whar a' the tones o' mis'ry's yell,
An' plagues in ranked numbers tell
    In deadly raw,
Thou, Tooth-ache, surely bear'st the bell
    Aboon them a'!

You can see that the iambic line is even at work here, through the shooting pains, carrying the poem along at a steady pace to its climax, where Burns wishes all Scotland's toothaches on her enemies, by which I assume he means the English.

Anything can be a sign or a signal: an internal discomfort, an animal that passes you on the road. Anything can serve your purpose here and offer a way of stepping outside yourself into something or someone else. This is the whole point of the pilgrimage: to allow yourself, through your new experiences, to become other than you are at home.

If you want to examine more of these amazing encounters, take a look at Jo Shapcott's 'Mad Cow' poems, where the poet becomes, in her poems, a mad cow herself, experiencing the explosive fizzing in the brain and the breaking down of conventional boundaries that are common both to disease and to the creative process. The poems enter into the crazy, broken places and, through the generosity and acceptance of metaphor, begin to heal them.

It is by approaching every encounter in a loving, accepting way that you will make the most powerful poems. Refusal and resistance will limit your powers of observation and your ability to make metaphorical connections. Look, feel, take in and write. You are whatever you look at, and everything has its own unique value.

Even a louse. On a serious pilgrimage you may well encounter a louse in some well-used bedding. Well, they have a right to be there too, and could well require their own poem. Here's Robert Burns again, in part of 'To A Louse, on seeing one on a lady's bonnet at church':

Ye ugly, creepin, blastit wonner,
Detested, shunn'd, by saunt and sinner,
How daur ye set your foot upon her,
    Sae fine a Lady!
Gae somewhere else and seek your dinner,
    On some poor body.

Don't be shy about having a bit of an argument with whatever you're looking at. Everything we see triggers complex responses because it evokes a web of memories and feelings. And because we tend to make connections all the time, even the sight of something completely new will remind you of things you already know. That's why metaphor is so important, forming a bridge between the known and the unknown. So if you meet a camel or a louse on your way, talk to it and tell it what it reminds you of. In each encounter a whole world will unfold, as it unfolds under your feet while you walk along.

What do you think of the path you are walking? Is it your own country or are you a foreigner here? Are you at home, or not? You can investigate your feelings about the land you are walking through to great effect, as R.S. Thomas did in his poem 'Welsh', published in 1961. Here is part of it:

> I want my own
> Speech, to be made
> Free of its terms.
> I want the right word
> For the gut's trouble,
> When I see this land
> With its farms empty
> Of folk, and the stone
> Manuscripts blurring
> In wind and rain.

Thomas has certainly broken the back of the pentameter here. If the iambic line bears the brand of the invading forces, Thomas has found a way of getting free of it. Though he's stuck with English, his adopted tongue, he can at least break with its conformities and so express his longing for a language – Welsh – which was taken from him at birth.

As you walk, consider these questions in yourself. How at ease do you feel in this landscape and this language? Do you long for somewhere else, or to express yourself in some other way? If the iambic line is beginning to bother you and make you feel restricted, shorten it, as Thomas has, or make it as long as you like, as the poet C.K. Williams does. Don't allow it to outlive its usefulness.

And if, when you reach your place of pilgrimage, you find it hideously commercialized, then light out for the territory ahead, as Huck Finn did, and make a dash for your own holy place. One of the poets in a poetry group made the journey to Walsingham and found it appalling, and so began her pilgrimage by trying to walk as far away from it as possible. That, too, will make a good poem. She walked for twenty miles before she found a bus-stop, however, which might serve as a warning to plan your journey before you start, rather than being forced to spend the night in a wet ditch. That might bring a poem but also, perhaps, a spell in Accident and Emergency. Anything serves, but the main thing, if you're going to become a good poet, is to keep yourself alive.

COMING HOME

What is it like to return home after a pilgrimage? What have you gained, what have you left along the way? As you reach home and cease walking, feel the change of rhythm within your body as you begin to settle down, greet the

45

familiar, relax and take a drink or a bath. These responses may be complex, so be as free as you like in your observations. Range at will over the page, as Adrienne Rich did in her poem 'Children Playing Checkers at the Edge of the Forest', published in 1987.

> But you're not playing, you're talking
>> It's midsummer
> and greater rules are breaking
>> It's the last
> innocent summer you will know
>> and I
> will go on awhile pretending that's not true

This is a portion of a longer poem, which addresses itself to questions of innocence and experience. And, as every journey changes us, you yourself will have brought your own new internal landscape home with you, the different stations that you now need to integrate into the more permanent station which is your home. It's in this poem that you bring your new experience into the realm of home that is, as yet, innocent of what you've been through. Because the pilgrimage is no longer out there, on the road, it's now in here, inside yourself, and needs to be acknowledged as part of you by courtesy of words on paper. In this poem you bring the natural world of the pilgrimage into the sanctuary of home, as you would bring home beautiful stones from a holiday to keep on a table. The poem is evidence that you've not returned empty-handed: you've brought something back.

COUNTING YOUR TREASURES

When you've been back about a week, gather all your nature poems together and look at them with a cool eye. Again, as with the poems in Chapter 1, be aware of the words and phrases that leave you feeling exhilarated, more alert and vigilant, and the ones that leave you feeling flat or with a sense of 'So what?' These latter will be the parts that require the transformation of metaphor or, more simply, an unexpected word that lifts the poem out of mere description into some new connection.

If you can, leave the poems out on a table so you can return to them over the next few days and make any changes you need to as they come to you. And when they're as ready as they can be for now, key them in on the computer so you can see what they look like in the more formal attire of print. Do this with your 'Origins' poems too, but be sure to put them in a different folder, and date them so you can access them again easily. Putting dates on your poems also enables you to see the way your writing has developed over a period of time.

Count your poems. How many do you have now?

Some seeds grow into plants, some into children and some into poems. Nature is never spent.

3 LOVE POEMS

Now may be the first moment since the beginning of time when we are able to begin to write real love poems. Why? Because for the first time in history, at least in our own little privileged enclave in the Western world, the conditions have started to exist for people to experience relationships of equality.

What are these conditions? Well, first of all, financial independence. If one person has to depend on another financially, the chances are that they will not feel free to make their own choices without feeling beholden in some way to the one who gives them sustenance. The second is the control of fertility. If one partner is continually bearing children, her body gradually exhausted by the demands of the next generation, then the leisure for feelings of love, let alone their expression in poems, simply does not exist.

So what about all the great love poems of the past? These pave the way for the poems that we now may begin to write, because all existing love poems emerge from places of inequality and impossibility. In the past, with its huge differences of wealth and the dangers of childbirth, love between equals was an absolute rarity. So what was celebrated was unrequited love, courtly love, impossible love.

We still have that legacy today, and we tend to celebrate impossible love over everyday love. Indeed, we may find it difficult to imagine love emerging out of everyday things, out of cooking and eating together, bathing a child together, taking care of each other in old age. However, the conditions of life have changed and will continue to change, and what seemed impossible in the past may be eminently possible now.

What I want to do now is to take you through some of the great love poems that have come down to us, so you can make up your own mind about what was and what was not possible to the men and women who wrote them, and decide for yourself, too, whether it is now possible to celebrate equal love between human beings. And while we are doing these things, we will try our hands at the sestina, the sonnet and a form called the 'pantoum', all of which have been used to write love poems.

First, we will look at one of the poems of Rumi, who has been estimated to be the most well-loved poet in the world at present. His poems are read by people of all faiths as well as those with no faith, providing a heart-stirring delight and self-questioning that leave the reader in a state of joyous not-knowing. Rumi himself was born in what is now Afghanistan in 1207, but his family moved to Turkey around 1215 to escape from the threat of the invading Mongol armies. His father was a mystical theologian and jurist, and Rumi's own life seems to have been one of a religious scholar, until one day in the autumn of 1244 when a stranger named Shams (which means 'the sun') asked Rumi a question about the prophet Muhammad, and Rumi was so overwhelmed by its depth of wisdom that he fell to the ground. After that they were inseparable. Rumi and Shams were always together, to the detriment of Rumi's family and students, locked in a mystical conversation where the individual selfhood of both seemed to disappear, and they became one.

Rumi doesn't seem to have written poems about his love until the pressure of jealousy from his students and family became so great that Shams left Turkey. Rumi then became a poet and began to sing, whirling around, the first whirling dervish. This poem shows something of his sense of their merging together, and merging, too, into God and the whole created universe.

The Shape of My Tongue

This mirror inside me shows ...
I can't say what, but I can't not know!

I run from body. I run from spirit.
I do not belong anywhere.

I'm not alive!
You smell the decay?

You talk about my craziness,
Listen rather to the honed-blade sanity I say.

This gourd head on top of a dervish robe,
do I look like someone you know?

This dipper gourd full of liquid,
upside down and not spilling a drop!

Or if it drops, it drops into God
and rounds into pearls.

I form a cloud over that ocean
and gather spillings.

When Shams is here,
I rain.

After a day or two, lilies sprout,
the shape of my tongue.

> The Essential Rumi, *trans. Coleman Barks with John Moyne (Penguin, 1995)*

In the poem, as in all experience of intense love, everything is turned upside down. Death becomes life and madness becomes sense. The overturned gourd either does not spill, or its liquid becomes precious pearls.

Do you know this feeling of confusion and merging, or can you imagine it? It may not be so very different from the writing you did in the last chapter, where you concentrated on merging with an object in Nature. Here, you are merging with an object, too, but here your object is the love object, the beloved. For Rumi, the earthly beloved and the divine Beloved were essentially the same: he reached the divine through his experience of human love. But whether or not you yourself believe this, you may still concede that love changes everything: the way we feel in our bodies, how we sleep, how the world looks to us when we open our eyes, and whether life itself seems to be worth living. In Oliver Sachs' *Awakenings*, about the experience of people with sleeping sickness, he calls Eros 'the oldest and strongest god', capable of sustaining people through terrible pain and suffering.

MYSTICAL CONVERSATION

I want you now to try your hardest poem so far, which is to be a description, in unrhyming couplets (as is Rumi's) of this love, this state of undoing that seems to unpick everything we've been before and re-weave us in new, unrecognizable clothing. One woman said to me that when she was first in love she noticed that people seemed to rush to sit near her on the Underground. As if love gave off a scent that others wanted to breathe in, as if people wanted to be close to the experience of love. As if they hungered for it, like a birthright.

Don't count syllables or worry about metre. Just let it come as you remember or imagine it. How does it make you feel? What does it look like? How does it sound, taste, smell and feel? Love is an abstract word. We can't see it, so we have to give it a body, and this body may be the body of the beloved: the beloved becomes a metaphor for love itself. Or perhaps, as in Rumi's poem, aspects of Nature become metaphors for the experience: the whole universe is the canvas whereon he paints his sufferings and his ecstasy.

Why couplets? Because you do well to allow your poem to reflect and embody all the aspects of your theme. In Dante's *Divine Comedy*, everything comes in threes: the Father, Son and Holy Ghost; Heaven, Hell and Purgatory;

the Poet, Beatrice and God. Dante invented a form, the terza rima, that would reveal the tripartite nature of the realities he was exploring. Here, on the other hand, it all comes in twos: you and the beloved; before and after love; hope and despair; illusion and disillusion. The lover's world is an experience of duality which is straining towards unity. The couplet, therefore, can help you to struggle with the paradox of love, as you try to represent the conversation between lover and beloved, their experiences of merger and their separations back into their individual identities.

Now write it. Sit down wherever you are and write it.

Rumi lost Shams. Although Shams returned after his first departure, the jealousies soon started to fester again. There's a saying that all the world loves a lover. Well, this evidently wasn't true in the case of Rumi and Shams because, although no trace was found of his body, just a line of blood in the sand, it seems that Shams was murdered by a member of Rumi's family. Afterwards, Rumi's poems developed out of his friend's absence, the absence giving them their intense longing and power.

THE ABSENT BELOVED

Rumi died in 1273, and a little later, in 1304 in Arezzo, Italy, his family having been exiled from Florence, Petrarch was born. Although Petrarch spent most of his life studying sacred and classical literature and trying to conquer the desires of his own senses, when he died he left behind a volume of work called the Canzoniere. These poems were written in Italian rather than Latin, and explored Petrarch's love for Laura, a woman with whom he seems never to have had a physical relationship, and towards whom the poems show an intense and unrequited love.

We know that Laura died around 1348, perhaps as a victim of the plague, and her death seems to have inspired yet more poems. Petrarch's love poetry, then, like Rumi's, arises out of the absence of the beloved, an attempt to honour and hold them in words when they are no longer present in the flesh.

Here is the twenty-second poem of the Canzoniere, which is a sestina.

For any animal that lives on earth,	1
except for those few that hate the sun,	2
the time to toil is while it is still day;	3
but then when heaven lights up all its stars	4
some go back home while some nest in the wood	5
to find some rest at least until the dawn.	6
And I, from the first signs of lovely dawn	6
shaking the shadows from around the earth	1
awakening the beasts in every wood,	5
can never cease to sigh while there is sun;	2
then when I see the flaring of the stars	4
I start to weep and long for the gone day.	3

When night drives out the clarity of day	3
and our darkness brings out another's dawn,	6
I gaze all full of care at the cruel stars	4
that once created me of sentient earth,	1
and I curse the first day I saw the sun	2
which makes me seem a man raised in the wood.	5
I think there never grazed in any wood	5
so cruel a beast, whether by night or day,	3
as she for whom I weep in shade and sun,	2
from which I am not stopped by sleep or dawn;	6
for though I am a body of this earth,	1
my firm desire is born from the stars.	4
Before returning to you, shining stars,	4
or sinking back into the amorous wood*	5
leaving my body turned to powdered earth,	1
could I see pity in her, for one day	3
can restore many years, and before dawn	6
enrich me from the setting of the sun!	2
Could I be with her at the fading sun	2
and seen by no one, only by the stars,	4
for just one night, to never see the dawn	6
and she not be transformed into green wood*	5
escaping from my arms as on the day	3
Apollo had pursued her here on earth!**	1
But I'll be under earth in a dry wood	1–5
and day will be all full of tiny stars	3–4
before so sweet a dawn will see the sun.	6–2

Petarch, Selections from the Canzoniere and Other Works, trans. Mark Musa (OUP)

* According to Virgil, the 'amorous wood' is the place in the Underworld assigned to those who die for love.
** These lines refer to the myth of Daphne and Apollo. The 'green wood' is probably a reference to the laurel tree. The latin word 'laurus' was believed to derive from the word 'laudare', to praise. It was considered to be the crown of poets and emperors.

As you can see, there are six and a half verses here, and the last word in each line recurs in a different place in every verse. In the last three lines of the poem, called the envoi, the signing-off, we see these words in a different order again. There are ten syllables in each line (although many contemporary poets don't stick to this) and you don't have to worry about rhyme, only about getting the correct word at the end of each line. Only!

This may well seem to you to be the strangest verse-form you've encountered: more of a crossword-puzzle than a poem. But I think you'll discover, once you begin, that the demands of the end-words take you into territory you didn't know you wanted to explore, surprising you into new paths, into thoughts and feelings you didn't know you had.

You can approach the sestina in at least two ways. Either write the first verse as you want to and then follow the formula for the changing order of end-words as I've indicated in the Petrarch poem. Or, if you want to throw your poem upon the whims of Mistress Fortune, deal yourself a hand of six cards, six end-words, and write them at the ends of the lines in the order I've indicated – and then write your poem with each line leading towards the word that's waiting for it at the end. Either is good.

You may think at first that this verse form is too formulaic and will allow you no freedom, but give it a chance. Once you've got to know it, you'll find that it gives you more room to manoeuvre than you imagined. It can be a fun game, because it invites you to contemplate your subject in the spirit of play and so lighten your mind of its burden of thought, so new images can come in.

Some writers have complained to me that there's no logic to a sestina. They can see the point in writing a sonnet, because it has a problem and a solution; it makes sense. But a sestina makes no kind of sense. If you feel like this about it, try looking at it as a series of reflecting mirrors which enable you to see your subject from different angles. Or as that old rippled glass that, when you look through it, makes you see the outside world differently depending on which part of the window you are looking through. Each verse is a different part of the window glass and, as you look through each part, you get a new vantage point, a new angle of vision.

Just in case you doubt that the sestina ever made it to the twenty-first century, I'm including two more that were written recently by friends of mine. Both are love poems, and both friends moaned interminably about having to write them. But as you can see, the form took them into memories and details that perhaps surprised them. You never know how far you can go until you follow the path that the six words take you down.

Our Drab Rug

The rationed rug wool came in wartime shades.
In an October letter you list the choice:
saxe-blue or pink or drab? You favoured drab.
What size of rug? And did she want a pattern?
From hospital you wrote; drew stiff blooms half
across the page. Something useful for the home,

because, once well, you would be back at home.
Bed rest behind redundant blackout shades,

recuperating for the other half
of your yet-tender life, and all the choices
of post-war London; setting a pattern
for our family life around a drab

hearthrug. Made by Dad. Victorious drab!
Exuberant hue of our united home.
For our hearthrug, we would not want a pattern
which soon would date. We would prepare for shades
of the new decade: contemporary choices
for the four Wardmans in the second half

of the twentieth century. A brighter half,
a brighter hearth, and soon we'd learn that drab
was beige and earth and camel and the choice
of style. The atmosphere and flavour of our home
would be a blend of both our parents, shades
of difference, clashing, then settling into a pattern.

And then you died, and left your girls no pattern.
Just a plain drab hearthrug only half
completed. As nineteen forty-six shaded
into forty seven, she finished off the drab
rectangle for you. For us. For our home.
For with the shortages, she had no other choice.

You could not see the join. What other choice
but put us into care? Thus was her pattern
for our life set, and with her alone at home.
We lost our mum, our other parent half,
so parented each other in that drab
institution. And now for her the shades

have drawn down. We will never know which half
was worked by each. But I can wrap that drab
old rug around me. And there is a pattern.

Penny Wardman Solomons

Notice the constantly shifting meanings of the words at the end of each line, especially the word 'drab', that the poet has infused with such depth and poignancy that it seems to me impossible to use it without thinking of how hard and usefully it worked in this poem.

The next poem is very different, but here again the meanings shift and flit about. And the poet has with amazing bravery used the word 'medina' as one of her end-words, showing that it doesn't matter how unusual your six words

may be. If you use them skilfully they will reveal deeper and deeper levels of
their meaning.

Painting in Henna

You say you want to return here to live, to get back your life
as a painter. I know you miss the wonderful light.
In spite of the heat you hold my hand.
'I have lived too long,' you tell me, 'in a country so dark
the promises I made to myself have been broken.
One day I will return, find somewhere in the medina.'

Today everywhere is closed and quiet in the medina
where people on their way to the mosque are the only signs of
      life.
It is the Prophet's birthday, and certain rules must not be broken.
I wait for you, drifting in and out of my book, until the fading
      light
beckons us into the soft air between dusk and dark.
We walk to the café in the Boulevard, not touching, not walking
      hand in hand.

The frail young man near us is so handsome.
I noticed him earlier making painful progress across the square
      in the medina.
He sits alone, but at all the other tables in this crowded dark
space, he is surrounded by men, their voices full of life,
their interaction easy and lighthearted.
It is a cruel contrast to a spirit that already seems broken.

'Why do you look so sad?' you ask, 'so heartbroken?
Some day we will all pass away. It is in God's hands.'
I am pestered by an insolent-eyed boy selling Marlboro Lights.
'Go away,' you shout, and he scuttles down an alley towards the
      medina.
'Why be upset by these things. Here, they are part of life.'
Your smile is lost in this smoke-filled darkness.

I lie awake that night, wondering why you choose to keep me in the
      dark,
rarely mention your family. I know so little about your broken
marriage and the daughter that was once part of your life.
You miss her, I know, but her future seems out of your hands.
I am haunted by your words in the medina,
words I feel that I should not pass over lightly.

We walk to your favourite beach in dazzling sunlight
where we feast on grilled fish and olives, sitting in the cool dark
shade of overhanging rocks. Later you will take me back to the
　　medina
to find the old woman who lives somewhere near the broken-
down cinema and ask her to paint in henna on my feet or hands:
a design that celebrates life.

With deft stokes, she lightly draws fine lines, broken
up by strange dark symbols on the palm of my hand.
She says they will protect me after I leave the medina, protect me all my
　　life.

Joyce Goldstein

The sestinas of Petrarch, Goldstein and Solomons all deal in some way with absence: the absence of the beloved or that of the beloved place, the home place. But what would it be like, do you think, to celebrate the beloved in the present, without idealization, in all his or her glorious particularity? In one of Sappho's poems, written in the fifth century BCE, she is addressing the question of what is the most beautiful sight on earth, and she says something like: 'Some say it is an army with banners, but I say it is what one loves.' What or whom do you love so much that you think of them as the most beautiful sight on earth? Write down the first six words you think of, the words you always associate with them. Now begin your first sestina.

Try to write your first draft all in one piece, without interruption. It's a long poem, and could take you some time, but why not? People spend their time doing far more ridiculous things. Your boss may be hassling you to finish a report, or your kids may be asking you to make supper. Your reply is: in a while. It can wait. I'm writing a sestina. They'll hoot with derision at first, but in the end they'll come to understand that poems need to be written, too, and sometimes they have to come before work or food. Because poems are a different kind of work, a different kind of food.

After you've written the sestina, put it away in the drawer until the end of the chapter. You need to let it sit and not attack it immediately. I find that the destructive critical voices in our heads are most audible just after the poem's been written (you have, after all, changed the world by adding something new to it, and there are parts of us that are very conservative, very resistant to anything new), whereas if you come back to it later, you're calmer, less anxious, because you can already see the poem as separate from yourself, with its own needs and requirements. It is these you will address when the time comes, rather than the irrelevant noises of your own self-criticism. The critical noises are part of you, not part of the poem, so you need to give them time to simmer down before we come to the important work of revision.

A Rest from Form

I find that prescribed forms tend to alternate, in my own poems, with freer ones – as if the tendons and muscles of poetry needed to tense and loosen, tense and loosen. Or as if the form is a breathing in, a filling up with experience acquired from the past, and the free verse is an expiration, a relieved letting-go into the unknown world of the present. But a letting-go that carries the wisdom of the past with it, too.

> The existing order is complete before the new work arrives; for order to persist after the supervention of novelty, the whole existing order must be, if ever so slightly, altered; and so the relations, proportions, values of each work of art toward the whole are readjusted; and this is conformity between the old and the new. Whoever has approved this idea of order ... will not find it preposterous that the past should be altered by the present as much as the present is directed by the past. And the poet who is aware of this will be aware of great difficulties and responsibilities ...
>
> Someone said: 'The dead writers are remote from us because we know so much more than they did.' Precisely, and they are that which we know.
>
> T.S. Eliot, 'Tradition and the Individual Talent' in *The Sacred Wood* (1920)

What I'd like you to consider now, as subject matter, is an artefact belonging to someone you love or have strong feelings about. This artefact (a shoe, a hair-slide, a cuff-link, a tooth) will take you into memories you perhaps thought you had lost or left behind. Let the artefact take you into your labyrinth of thoughts about this person, knowing that the poem will take you out again when you've completed your exploration.

You might like to take a look first at this poem by Hart Crane, from his first collection *White Buildings* (Boni & Liveright, 1926). Crane had a complicated and painful relationship with his family, which may finally have played its part in his death by drowning in 1932, but in this poem there's an inclusion and generosity that reveals a desire 'to carry back the music to its source'. Finding the source of the music is your aim in this poem. Whether the music is harmonious, harsh and strident, or barely audible, it is the unique music of your own love, and the artefact will take you near to it and enable you to hear it.

My Grandmother's Love Letters

There are no stars to-night
But those of memory.
Yet how much room for memory there is
In the loose girdle of soft rain.

There is even room enough
For the letters of my mother's mother
Elisabeth,
That have been pressed so long
Into a corner of the roof
That they are brown and soft,
And liable to melt as snow.

Over the greatness of such space
Steps must be gentle.
It is all hung by an invisible white hair.
It trembles as birch limbs webbing the air.

And I ask myself:

'Are your fingers long enough to play
Old keys that are but echoes:
Is the silence strong enough
To carry the music to its source
And back to you again
As though to her?'

Yet I would lead my grandmother by the hand
Through much of what she would not understand;
And so I stumble. And the rain continues on the roof
With such a sound of gently pitying laughter.

Let your lines be as long or as short as they want to be. Listen for the music of each line, guided by the words of Crane's poem when he says 'Over the greatness of such space / Steps must be gentle.' The artefact is your bridge between the past and the present, an object that literally belongs to the beloved, but which also stands as a symbol of their living presence. It brings what is past and gone into the here and now, as the poem itself also does. But it's the object that enables you to write the poem.

Listen, too, for the rhythm inherent in the object. Is it the walking feet you used in the pilgrimage poem, or the faster, more energetic pace of the trochaic foot, which has alternating strong and weak beats, with each line bursting into view with a stressed syllable, like this: ONE two, ONE two, ONE two? Or is it the dactyl, which dances along like a waltz (ONE two three, ONE two three, ONE two three), or the anapaest, rattling along like a machine, or a machine gun (one two THREE, one two THREE, one two THREE). You won't stick to any of these throughout the whole poem, but you may find that one occurs more often than the rest, and this will reveal to you the kind of energy that lies inherent in the object.

Now settle yourself in a quiet place to write your poem. Place the object close to you or, if you don't physically have it with you, close to you in your mind. Allow yourself to dream it. Where did you first encounter it? What are the thoughts, feelings and images that begin to congregate around it? Let them come. Welcome them. They are telling you how to begin your poem.

And when you've written your poem, put it away until later.

DOING THE BUSINESS WITH THE SONNET

Now that you've strengthened yourself with couplets, a sestina and some free verse, it's time to take on the sonnet. The big one. This is the form that has persisted and challenged poets most strongly since its invention, which may have been in Sicily in the eleventh century. So much love poetry, in different forms, but often in the sonnet form, was written around this time, that we are forced to wonder why this flowering occurred. The American poet Robert Bly, in his anthology *The Rag and Bone Shop of the Heart* (Harper Perennial, 1992), argues that a religion of love, AMOR, emerged at that time, in response to the orthodox Christianity of Rome. AMOR, he points out, is ROMA, but backwards.

Love and orthodox religious belief have often sat uneasily together. Petrarch couldn't reconcile the desires of his senses with his spiritual yearnings, construing the body as something soiled, an indication of our fallen state. And perhaps the most dramatic moment in this conflict is the experience of Abelard and Heloise, who tried to combine carnal and spiritual love, and, because of the punitive conventions of medieval society, failed tragically.

Abelard was a monk and a philosopher at the height of his powers, aged nearly forty, when he fell in love with his pupil Heloise, who was eighteen. She became pregnant and he wanted to marry her, but she refused, believing that domestic life and children spelled death for philosophy: that body–mind divide again! They ran away from Italy together and lived in Paris. Heloise's father then sent a servant after Abelard, who gained entry into his bedchamber and castrated him. After that, Abelard retired to a monastery and commanded Heloise to do the same. Ten years later, when he had become an abbot and she an abbess, she wrote to him, saying that her desires were the same, and that she would rather be Abelard's 'strumpet' than God's servant. His reply, rather conventionally and disappointingly, was that they would meet again in heaven.

But Joseph Campbell, the great writer on myth and religion, has cited Heloise's letter as the first moment when a person raised their own authority, the desires of their own heart, over the authority of the Church. Someone has to do it first. Someone has to say 'I feel this, no matter what the rules are', and, although Heloise wrote a letter, it's often the poets who say it first – perhaps because they think they are ignored anyway, and that nobody is listening to them.

Perhaps we could say that the courtly love poets of the middle ages occupied a kind of half-way house, where human love was longed for but not, at that stage, possible. Where the woman was idealized, distant and spiritual, and the lover saw himself as her servant. Apart from Heloise's letter, there seems to be no evidence of a person displaying an intention, or a wish, to act out their desires and own and acknowledge the longings of their heart and their senses.

Of course, we have no record of what the lower orders were getting up to, but I suspect they were far more sensible. It's a great pity that most of them didn't read or write, and that the idealized women, the objects of desire in the courtly love poems, also kept quiet about how they felt about all this.

SPEAKING FOR THE SILENT ONES

But perhaps we can help them to speak now. I want you to look at a very famous sonnet by Sir Thomas Wyatt. It may well have been inspired by an earlier sonnet by Petrarch, where the poet follows a beautiful deer, wears himself out in the pursuit, and finally falls into a pond. Wyatt's may refer to his involvement with Ann Boleyn, which seems to have cost him some time in the Tower of London.

Whoso list to hunt, I know where is an hind,	A
But as for me, helas! I may no more.	B
The vain travail hath wearied me so sore,	B
I am of them that furthest come behind.	A
Yet may I, by no means, my wearied mind	A
Draw from the deer; but as she fleeth afore	B
Fainting I follow. I leave off therefore	B
Since in a net I seek to hold the wind.	A
Who list her hunt, I put him out of doubt,	C
As well as I, may spend his time in vain;	D
And graven with diamonds in letters plain	D
There is written, her fair neck round about,	C
'Noli me tangere, for Caesar's I am,	E
And wild for to hold, though I seem tame.'	E

This sonnet follows a rhyme-scheme that came to us from Italy, which is indicated by the capital letters at the end of each line. Can you see how tight the rhymes are, how in the octave (the first eight lines) you have only two rhymes, which are each repeated four times? This may be much easier in Italian, where many words end in a vowel sound, and so lend themselves more readily to rhyme. But in English, you may say to yourself: how am I to do it? Well, remember that English has more words than all the Romance languages put together, so you have many more to choose from. The American poet Marilyn Hacker has pointed out that you can rhyme Anglo-Saxon and Latinate words together, verbs with nouns, words of many syllables with words of one, the learned or the lyrical with the everyday, with obscene words, and with dialect. Our language is so rich because of all the past invasions (the Romans, the Angles and the Saxons, the Vikings, the Normans) and because of the enriching streams of immigration that constantly bring in new words. Language is a mysterious river, like the Nile. Its flow brings rich deposits from upstream, where the Mountains of the Moon slowly release their volcanic fertility. The words are always there, plenty of them, more than enough; it's just a question of waiting for them to come to you, or wading out into the river to find them.

But before you try your own sonnet, let's take a close look at Thomas Wyatt's. Traditionally, the Italian sonnet presents some kind of problem in the octave, which is resolved in the sestet, the last six lines. Is this the case here? I don't think it is. If anything, the problem deepens. The poet gets more and more tired following this wretched deer, and finally warns anyone else who might fancy taking up the chase that she belongs to Caesar anyway, and she's got a collar round her neck to prove it.

You might think, Tom, isn't the deer metaphor is a bit obvious? Won't you get into trouble at court if your sonnet falls under the gaze of Henry VIII? And is she worth the trouble anyway? Plenty more pebbles on the beach. Why worry about this one?

Poets do tend to take crazy risks when they are living under tyrants. The Russian poet Osip Mandelstam was eventually sent to Siberia, and died there, for a poem about Stalin that he read out to a room of ten people. Osip! Don't do it! You know what's going to happen to you! It wasn't even a great poem, unlike the rest of his *oeuvre* – but some poets, it seems, will risk everything for love, whether for an individual or for their country.

My own view is that poets should write poems and take care, rather than dying for an idea or a cause. Tyrants come and go, but poetry doesn't choose everybody to flow through. It only chooses a few, and those few should take care of themselves so the poems can continue to flow. The Chilean poet Pablo Neruda is one who held passionate convictions but still managed to stay alive, at least until General Pinochet came to power.

But, looking at Wyatt's poem again, I can see a kind of turn (*volta* in Italian) when the poet decides simply to stop chasing:

> I leave off therefore
> Since in a net I seek to hold the wind.

He then turns to an imaginary audience of the woman's other admirers and advises them not to waste their time, since she's not free to give her favours to anyone but the king. And he rounds off the sonnet with a rhyming couplet that prepares us for the way Shakespeare dramatized the form with his wonderful heroic couplets.

You may notice that in this poem the deer has nothing whatever to say for herself. The poet speaks, and Caesar has put his mark on her, but she herself is completely silent. How do you think she feels about all this hunting, all this rush to possess her? How would you feel? Let it all collect inside you. Remember that, until well into the nineteenth century, a man could imprison his wife at home if she tried to run away from him. Women couldn't own property, their children belonged to their husbands, and they couldn't elect representatives to govern them until 1921. Potential equality is very recent, and still exists only in certain parts of the world. Wyatt was writing at a time when there was absolutely none.

Imagine being the king's creature. What would she say, if she could find the words? What would she be afraid to say, but let slip anyway? How would her thoughts move, how would they dodge about? Would she speak plainly or furtively? Would she equivocate? Would her words be deliberately ambiguous?

Go to your table now and begin your sonnet. Don't concern yourself about the rhymes at first. If they come, they come. If not, no matter. You don't want to sacrifice the essence of what you're writing for a rhyme. But do try to keep to ten syllables in each line, and present the reader with a problem which may or may not have a solution. And remember – fourteen lines. You'll find that this form, though it may seem to constrain you at first, will finally lead you into images and thoughts that emerge as entirely new, that you didn't know, consciously, were there inside you, waiting to come out.

All the poetic forms enable what was hidden inside to make an entry into the world, but the sonnet especially – else why would it have persisted so long, and have been so widely used, and so much loved?

When your first sonnet is finished (or the first draft anyway), give yourself a good pat on the back and put it away. You've achieved a great deal by even attempting the form, which holds within itself the shape of perfection, divided into a landscape format with its 8–6 division, embodying the Golden Mean. (If you see the sonnet as a picture, it is a landscape where the horizon is almost two thirds down the page.)

You've also given voice to something or someone who is silent, thus helping to balance the weight of words in the world.

BALANCING THE WORDS

When you have recovered from your sonnet-work, you can relax by experimenting with another verse form, the 'glose', Spanish this time. This one also takes the form of a response, but here you have complete freedom in how you write it. Each experiment with poetic form strengthens, focuses and sharpens your free verse, so it is a good idea to alternate them so that you can reap the benefit.

First, take four lines written by a poet to whom you respond strongly and put them at the top of your own poem as a kind of epigraph. Your own poem then becomes an explored answer to these four lines. In addition, these lines, one by one, should form the last lines of some of your own verses. You therefore integrate the other poet's lines into your own poem even while you are writing a response to them.

The four lines might not be from a poet you like or admire. You might think they are awful, and thoroughly disagree with them. So much the better. As long as your feelings are strong enough to start off your own poem, these will be the right four lines for you.

Now let yourself go – ranting, concurring, disagreeing, sympathizing, denouncing, as you wish. Let the poem be in free verse, and think of yourself in active dialogue with the four lines. Tell us what you really think, over as many verses as you like.

Now read your poem, and then put it away.

Lust and Love

I'd like us now to take a look at a sonnet by Shakespeare, which seeks to define an emotion that has always had a very bad press up to now. Christianity has traditionally seen lust as a sin, as Shakespeare does in this, one of his later sonnets.

Th' expense of spirit in a waste of shame	A
Is lust in action; and till action, lust	B
Is perjured, murd'rous, bloody, full of blame,	A
Savage, extreme, rude, cruel, not to trust;	B
Enjoy'd no sooner but despised straight;	C
Past reason hunted; and no sooner had,	D
Past reason hated, as a swallowed bait,	C
On purpose laid to make the taker mad:	D
Mad in pursuit, and in possession so;	E
Had, having, and in quest to have, extreme;	F
A bliss in proof, and proved, a very woe;	E
Before, a joy proposed; behind, a dream.	F
All this the world well knows; yet none knows well	G
To shun the heaven that leads men to this hell.	G

The rhyme-scheme I have shown on the right-hand side again, in capitals, so you can see how it works. Whereas the Italian sonnet is divided into two, and the sestet answers the problem laid down in the octave, here in the Shakespearean sonnet the logic works differently: the experience is explored literally and metaphorically, in all its many aspects, in alternating rhymes in the first twelve lines. Then the heroic couplet, the last two lines, provides a witty or reflective retort to all that has gone before. The Shakespearean sonnet winds the tension up higher than the Italian, and then releases it suddenly in the heroic couplet.

But what about what the sonnet says? Let's try to understand what Shakespeare wishes to communicate. It is part of a sequence of 150 sonnets, the earlier ones addressed to a beautiful young man whom Shakespeare urges to marry and have children so that his beauty will be passed down and not die with him. As the sequence progresses, a woman appears. She is not in the least an idealized figure, not a goddess. In fact, in two of the lines that praise her, Shakespeare says:

And in some perfumes there is more delight
Than in the breath that from my mistress reeks.

So she's a woman of the earth, and quite smelly too, though he doesn't seem to mind her smell. She also seems to be a liar, and the poet admits that he lies too when he's with her. They both lie, and they lie together. Then, in the sonnet 'Two loves have I of comfort and despair' there is an outburst of pain, that the dark lady is seducing the lovely young man away from him. He's not sure about this, and won't know for certain 'Till my bad angel fire my good one out.' The phrase 'to fire out' in Shakespeare's time meant to give someone venereal disease. So perhaps the poet is saying that he won't know that the young man has been seduced by 'my female evil' until he sees the signs of the pox on him. Or perhaps not. Perhaps 'my female evil' is a part of the poet himself, his own dark, not-fully-acknowledged, feminine side. We know very little about Shakespeare's life, and attempts to read actual events into poems often end in failure.

What does seem clear, though, is that the sonnet 'Th' expense of spirit' indicates a writer who's not easy with his own sexual desires. He seems to be saying that lust (a strong and judgmental word for desire) causes shame, which is a spending, or wasting, of the human spirit. And, if you don't enact this lust, it simmers inside in a dangerous way. If the lust is acted out, in other words by having sex with the person lusted after, this immediately leads you to despise that person and yourself. The pleasure is very brief, even though the lust that drove you to the act would have driven you mad if you had not submitted to it.

The poor man is damned if he does and damned if he doesn't. He even generalizes his own experience to include the whole world. Everyone, according to the sonnet, gets caught in the lust trap.

But is lust really so terrible? What do you think about lust and desire? A poet (I forget who) said 'Gluttony and sloth have often protected me from lust and anger.' But if you've not yet reached that sorry stage, spend some time noting down what it feels like to be overtaken by desire. How does it affect your appetite (for food), your breathing, how much you sweat, how you dress? How often do you think about the object of your desire? Do you ever not think about him or her? Do you enjoy desire, or do you wish it was over, that you were back to normal again? Do you feel bad about it, or does it enliven and exhilarate you? Or both? Write down everything you can think of about your feelings.

Now concentrate on the person you're lusting after. What do you think of that person? Do you admire, respect, or love that person, or is it all about sex? Or, as one man I knew rather vulgarly put it, 'I don't even fancy her, but I'd give her one.' Even lust, it appears, can sometimes be off-hand.

What is it about this person that obsesses (or, if it happened in the past, obsessed) you? A particular part of the body? The things they say? Is it their voice, the way they move, the way they make love, or lust?

Get it all down. This is your chance to begin to understand one of the most mysterious areas of our lives, one where (if Shakespeare is to be believed) we create big trouble for ourselves of our own free will, even though we may feel at every stage that we have no real choice in the matter. How often have you heard 'I couldn't stop, I had no choice' from people who in all other areas of their lives are perfectly thoughtful, rational human beings? Quite often, I'll bet. And you may feel sorry for them or make fun of them – until it happens to you. Then you find yourself the object of others' pitying gaze, and perhaps you feel rather humbled after that. Perhaps, then, you suddenly realize that there are limits to how much we are the masters of our own fate. Not just external limits (I can't be the Queen of England, no matter how hard I try) but internal limits, too (I can't get this person out of my head, no matter how hard I try). As Sir Thomas Wyatt said:

> Yet may I, by no means, my wearied mind
> Draw from the deer, but as she fleeth afore
> Fainting I follow...

And that's another thing about desire, isn't it? It makes you feel you're going to faint.

THE POEM OF DESIRE

Now sit down to write your own poem of desire. You've collected your thoughts on paper. Now ask yourself: is there a metaphor that holds all these thoughts together? Does an image come to mind? Perhaps yes, perhaps no. Thomas Wyatt had his deer, but Shakespeare's sonnet gives us no figurative language except for 'a swallowed bait' and 'a dream'. The rest of the poem uses abstract words like 'shame', 'reason' and 'pursuit'.

We wrestle with these abstractions in order to get to the heart of the poem. But if you have a metaphor that you wish to use, all the better, because this will take your reader into the thought process and argument of the poem more flowingly. We tend to think in pictures, even though we write in words. An image often used is that of water or drowning, bringing the feeling of being drowned in the water of desire.

When you've completed your first draft, read it and put it away.

After you've finished the first draft of your poem, you may find that you still have a lot more to say on the subject. In this case, let your thoughts and

An idea is derivative and tamed. The image is in the natural or wild state, and it has to be discovered there, not put there, obeying its own law and none of ours. We think we can lay hold of image and take it captive, but the docile captive is not the real image but only the idea, which is the image with its character beaten out of it ...

the image which is not remarkable in any particular property is marvellous in its assemblage of many properties, a manifold of properties, like a mine or a field, something to be explored for the properties; ...

People who are engrossed with their pet 'values' become habitual killers. Their game is the images, or the things, and they acquire the ability to shoot them as far off as they can be seen, and do. It is thus that we lose the power of imagination, or whatever faculty it is by which we are able to contemplate things as they are in their rich and contingent materiality. But our dreams reproach us, for in dreams they come alive again. Likewise our memory; which makes light of our science by recalling the images in their panoply of circumstance and with their morning freshness upon them.

John Crowe Ransom, 'Poetry: A Note In Ontology', in *The World's Body* (Charles Scribner's Sons, USA, 1938)

feelings pour into aphorisms, as William Blake's did in *The Marriage of Heaven and Hell.* Here are some of Blake's 'Proverbs of Hell' that relate in some way to the question of desire.

The road of excess leads to the palace of wisdom.

Prudence is a rich, ugly old maid courted by Incapacity.

He who desires but acts not, breeds pestilence.

The cut worm forgives the plow.

Dip him in the river who loves water.

The most sublime act is to set another before you.

If the fool would persist in his folly he would become wise.

Shame is Pride's cloke.

Prisons are built with stones of Law, Brothels with bricks of Religion.

The lust of the goat is the bounty of God.

The nakedness of woman is the work of God.

You never know what is enough unless you know what is more than enough.

As the caterpillar chooses the fairest leaves to lay her eggs on, so the priest lays his curse on the fairest joys.

Sooner murder an infant in its cradle than nurse unacted desires.

(Note that the unusual spelling is Blake's own.)

Don't you think these are amazing? Published in 1793, they go right against the teaching of the church and of established conventions – and against the argument in Shakespeare's sonnet, too. They throw off restrictions and place the joy of experience at the very centre of life. Do you agree with him? Think, now. When you look back over your own experience, what would be the proverbs, or aphorisms, that emerge as worth setting down for future reference? What are the sayings that come to you from your own life? Obviously they are unlikely to all come at once, so place a clean sheet of paper on your table and write them down as they float to the surface of your mind. Think of them as instructions, or lines of guidance, to yourself and those you love. Ask yourself: what have I learned about desire? How can I express it? How can I express it for the benefit of others? Give yourself a week on this exercise and then look at your harvest of sayings before putting them away.

DESIRE AND MEMORY

Here is an astonishing poem about the connections between desire and memory. It is by the British Afro-Caribbean poet Richard Dyer, and he uses the form of the 'pantoum'(originally, it's thought, a fishing song from the Far East, then taken up by French nineteenth-century poets) to explore the slow-moving nature of desire.

The Memory of Dolphins

Into the cool pool by moonlight
Stripped of code and clothes
To the intimacy of darkness
Our young skin moon-blind and watered.

Stripped of code and clothes
Naked as dreaming stone
Our young skin, moon-blind and watered
Makes us shiver, even in this heat.

Naked as dreaming stone
We become not human, this feeling
Makes us shiver, even in this heat
We move dolphin-wise as one.

We become not human, this feeling
Liquid as stars seen through wet eyes.
We move dolphin-wise as one
Causing a strange sound of water.

Liquid as stars seen through wet eyes
The leviathan movement of our back
Causing a strange sound of water
As our voices die to a whisper.

The leviathan movement of our back
Moving together as one form
As our voices die to a whisper
Beneath the gaze of an Argus moon.

Moving together as one form
Becoming the memory of dolphins
Beneath the gaze of an Argus moon
Churning the pool to a dark spasm.

Becoming the memory of dolphins
We separate, suddenly blind
Churning the pool to a dark spasm
Emerge into moon-dusk, then twist over.

We separate suddenly blind
To the intimacy of darkness
Emerge into moon-dusk, then twist over
Into the cool pool by moonlight.

Richard Dyer (originally published in Ambit *magazine)*

In the pantoum, you take lines 2 and 4 of the first verse and make them lines 1 and 3 of the second. Then lines 2 and 4 of the second verse become lines 1 and 3 of the third. Lines 2 and 4 of the third verse become lines 1 and 3 of the fourth – and so on. The final verse has to recapture the first verse by having, as its second and fourth lines, the third and first of verse one.

It sounds complicated, but can you see the effect it creates (rather like the 'terza rima' but more so)? It brings a slow swaying, constantly returning to the previous thought or image, so the reader's attention keeps moving forwards, then backwards, in a hypnotic, dizzying kind of movement.

It is the perfect form when you want to investigate images and feelings that return, move on, and change into different forms. A protean form, one that enables you to keep going back and watch as the old material from the past metamorphoses itself into new material in the present and the future.

Try it now for yourself. There are no rules apart from the ones just outlined. The lines can be any length, and there are no rhymes, so there's nothing to hold you back except for the repetition of lines two and four of each verse.

Think of a moment of terrific desire and give it to the reader in all its physical and emotional detail. Imagine the metaphor that emerges from it. (Dyer's controlling metaphor is the memory of dolphins, that inhuman-but-total communication that takes place between lovers, or between those who are following their desire to its culmination.) Allow your metaphor to weave itself into the details of your desire.

The key to the pantoum is flow. Let yourself flow into the body of your poem.

When you have completed the first draft, read it and then put it away.

DESIRE AND HATE

Do you find that it's hard to hold desire still, that it slips and slides into other feelings, sometimes, or perhaps especially, into hate?

What do you yourself want to say about the connections between desire and hate? Are they linked, do you think, and if so, how? The homeopathic doctor Alice Green in the book *Passionate Medicine* has talked about 'the distortions of love', and perhaps hate is one of these, emerging when love is rejected, or when it burns itself down to something else in acrimonious ways. Think about how close desire and hate are, and how quickly one can be transformed into the other.

Try your own poem now. Write it in whatever form you like, but write down what you want to say first, in prose. Madame Blavatsky advised the poet W.B. Yeats to do this. It makes your own thoughts clear to you before you start working on them as a poem. Afterwards, when you begin to consider rhythm, rhyme and metaphor, they will deepen into something beyond your original argument. But the first question is 'What do I want to say?'

When you've finished your extended aphorism, look at it without criticism or judgment (those can come later, with the clarity of distance) and then put it away with your others. Remember to divide your poems into sections: a folder for 'Origins', a folder for 'Nature Poetry' and one for 'Love Poetry'. And to put dates on your poems, too, so when you look back you can see how your work has developed.

The business of the poet is not to find new emotions, but to use the ordinary ones and, in working them up into poetry, to express feelings which are not in actual emotions at all ... There is a great deal, in the writing of poetry, which must be conscious and deliberate. In fact, the bad poet is unusually unconscious where he ought to be conscious, and conscious where he ought to be unconscious. Both errors tend to make him 'personal'. Poetry is not a turning loose of emotion, but an escape from emotion; it is not the expression of personality, but an escape from personality. But, of course, only those who have personality and emotions know what it means to escape from these things ...

The emotion of art is impersonal. And the poet cannot reach this impersonality without surrendering himself wholly to the work to be done. And he is not likely to know what is to be done unless he lives in what is not merely the present, but the present moment of the past, unless he is conscious, not of what is dead, but of what is already living.

T.S. Eliot, 'Tradition and the Individual Talent', in *Selected Essays* **(Harcourt, Brace & World Inc., USA, 1932)**

JEALOUSY

Jealousy may be another distortion of love, arising when love is divided, when one person feels they are having to share another. It can give rise to some marvellous metaphors – of jealousy as an animal that has to be kept locked up to protect the beloved from its destructive power, for example.

Here is a sonnet by Helena Nelson, whose first poetry collection *Starlight On Water* (The Rialto, 2003) won the Jerwood Aldeburgh First Collection Prize in 2003.

You've never seen my jealousy set loose
because I keep her chained. The place she sleeps
is deep and stone and chill. A brazen noose
encircles her hot throat – mostly it keeps
her teeth at bay. A daily douse of ice
prevents her blood from boiling. But her eyes
terrify most. They bleed with avarice.
She wants and wants and wants. No compromise.
She waits with deadly patience, knowing she
outlives most men. Her red hair seethes and glows,
filling the air with snakes. Resentfully
she squats and broods. Occasionally she grows.
No pet. You can neither tame nor breed her
And it isn't wise to – no – don't feed her.

Can you see how Helena Nelson plays with the fire/ice opposition, and the way she uses vowels and consonants that set your teeth on edge – loose/sleeps, noose/keeps, ice/eyes, avarice/compromise – giving you the feelings of intense discomfort that jealousy brings?

And is there something exciting, too, about this wild beast? That she could escape and attack the loved one, savaging him in an orgy of want? Perhaps jealousy is the other face of desire, a face that shows itself when the loved one is unavailable.

Choose now, whether to write your jealousy poem in a sonnet or free verse. If you chose free verse, think about the length of your lines. You may like to let each of them last for one short breath, so that the poem itself seems to be hyperventilating, breathing in that shallow, almost fainting way that comes when we're in the throes of a powerful feeling. In general, longer lines tend to give a sense of measure and control, while short ones take us straight into the feeling and hold us there. The short lines subvert the ironic tone of the poem, giving a sense of the pain that lies behind it.

Spend some time thinking back over all your experiences of jealousy, and choose one that seems to catch your own particular angle on this feeling.

Then begin your poem.

Once your draft is complete, put it away and then spend some time looking over this next (our last) sonnet. I find this one very special because of its mixture of self-love, love of team-mates, love of the crowd, and love, too, of the coach who trained her for this medal.

2003 – British Transplant Games

From the medal rostrum, my big lungs blow
a mistral that paints the cheering crowd
with an astonished victory grin. My brow

anoints the silver medal hanging proud
round my neck with golden sweat, fizzing
like shaken champagne popped with a bang as loud

as the starting gun which fanfared my sporting
dreams made real. My team-mates cheer with the wild
vitality of the reborn; whispering

cheers echo round the stadium sides,
our donors cock-a-hoop, trumping death. My
disbelieving coach, moustache split wide,

camera-captures the moment and our eyes
laser-link, holding ten breathless years
in one flash. We laugh. Huge, balloon-full cries
that burst with bronze, silver and gold.

Sandra Simmons

Sandra Simmons, as you might infer from the poem, is the recipient of a lung transplant. Before her operation she could move very little, never take a deep breath, and her fingernails were always blue. Throughout her life she had always treasured 'sporting dreams' and she always wore trainers because she saw herself as a sportswoman, but running was never possible until after her lung transplant.

I find this poem a quite different sort of love poem because of its delighted inclusiveness. Love radiates outwards from the poet's own self, with her strong new lungs – to her team-mates, the cheering crowd, then back to her coach with whom she exchanges a long look 'holding ten breathless years/in one flash.' There's no jealousy or competition for love here, although there has been a race: everyone is included in the joy.

Have you ever experienced anything like this, where differences are no longer important because of the love and joy of achievement? Perhaps it was an achievement that several of you experienced together, something collective, that went beyond individual boundaries; something you realized against great odds perhaps. Where you perceived that love is more widespread than you had thought, and that it doesn't just confine itself to two people.

Note down your recollections. This is a very special event, one where you stepped outside the restrictions of your own ego and glimpsed what it might be like to be a tribe, moving easily together towards a particular purpose. Society doesn't allow us many experiences like this, so it's as well to treasure the ones you've had, and keep a record that they happened.

Again, it's up to you to decide whether to write a sonnet or free verse. I think Sandra Simmons chose the sonnet because she wanted to hold the joy in a received form, to contain it in a beautiful container so it could be regarded and appreciated for its shape as well as for what it holds. You will have noticed, though, that she has overflowed her container: the sonnet is sixteen lines long. So feel free to break the bounds of the sonnet, too. Whether you hold the feeling firmly or loosely is up to you.

RE-VISION

We could go on writing about love and its distortions forever, but I think the time has come now to gather up all the poems in your Love Folder and look at them again. First of all, what do they tell you about yourself? One of the poet's tasks is to learn to know themselves, so they can understand more fully why they react to the world in the way they do. It can be very distracting when poets make broad generalizations about life which, when examined, prove to be merely projections of their own thought-forms, their own prejudices and obsessions. As you learn more about yourself through your poetry, you will gradually be able to get these out of the way so that the lens through which you see the world is clearer. Obviously we all project to a certain extent, but some prejudices (for example, the view that all marriages are unhappy) occlude your vision and prevent you from the aim that Virginia Woolf put forward: to see life steadily and see it whole.

So as you look at your love poems, be aware of your own particular angle of vision. Ask yourself 'Is there another way of seeing this? Can I imagine it any other way?' You may find that you can weave alternative possibilities into your poems and so endow them with irony, wit, a further dimension and depth.

When we speak of revision we sometimes automatically think of technical changes. The word 'technique' means 'making': how the poems are made. But they are made in a particular way because of how we see, feel and are in the world. So the most fundamental part of revision is just that: 're-vision', asking yourself to see your poem again, in a fuller, richer light.

If you look at early drafts of Wilfred Owen's poems, before Siegfried Sassoon got to work on them with him, or at T.S. Eliot's *The Waste Land* before it came under the cutting, revising pencil of Ezra Pound, you'll see that both poets suffered from a restricted vision which caught them in archaism and sentimentality. Sassoon and Pound forced them to see more clearly, to cut out anything Victorian or flowery, and enabled Owen and Eliot to enter into their full power as poets by helping them to let go of all that was not essential to their vision.

You may have a friend who can help you do this, but if not you can take comfort from the thought that your best friend, when revising your poems, is most probably yourself. So, after you've allowed your poems to lie fallow for a while in a drawer, take them out and look at them again. Let yourself re-envision them.

4 THE POETRY OF WAR

We saw the beginnings of war poetry in the last chapter, where we examined love poetry. Helena Nelson's 'Jealousy' sonnet showed how close the green-eyed monster can come when the beloved is blithely unaware of her. This is, as Alice Greene has explained, one of the distortions of love: love turning to hatred down the dark passageways of jealousy and rejection.

But this isn't war. This is merely personal conflict. So when does a personal conflict broaden into a war, and why should poets write about war when it happens? If nations are stupid enough to go to war, why not keep quiet about it until it's over, or write love poetry to drown out war's propaganda?

One answer seems to be that the experience of war takes us into the extremes of human feeling and behaviour, as does love, and if we are to begin to understand those feelings and actions we must write about them, because writing allows us to see them on the page before us: enables us, in some fundamental way, to see what we are doing.

And why war-*poetry*? Why not novels or plays or films about war? Well, all of these exist of course, but the human impulse to turn our experiences into song and so make a lasting record that sinks deep into the culture is very strong. When we think of the First World War we don't first think of the novelists or the playwrights: we think of the poets. It is the poets who get there first, as do the journalists, to help us see what is going on. It is the poets, like the journalists, who will go into the burning building to find out who lit the match and why, rather than running for cover.

And why do wars happen anyway? How can people be stupid enough to go out and kill one another *en masse*? The mythographer Joseph Campbell and the ethologist Jane Goodall both take the story back to our near cousins (we share 99% of our DNA with them): the chimpanzees. Joseph Campbell proposes that the task of the male chimps is to find food for the whole group. But when they know where all the bananas are (and they are almost as smart as we are, so it can't take that long), what are they to do next? Get bored, maybe. Maybe attack another group of chimps.

Jane Goodall watched the Gombe chimps for eleven years, and had begun to believe that they had brought their aggressive instincts under control with complicated rituals of submission, hugging and reconciliation. Then, overturning her admiration into horror, they went to war with another group. And what did they do during this war? They killed one another, took prisoners, slaughtered and cannibalized babies, turning into monstrous versions of themselves. As we do.

What shall we make of this? That war-making is hard-wired into the human brain?

There is a theory (supported by the novelist Arthur Koestler) that, because the brains of human beings contain the traces of the brains of all our evolutionary ancestors (fish, reptiles, rabbits etc.) at the back of our skulls, as well as the beguilingly clever neo-cortex at the front, these two types of thinking tend to interfere with and confuse each other. The *medulla oblongata*, at the back, tells us to either submit or retreat from danger when we are faced with an enemy stronger than ourselves. The *neo-cortex*, on the other hand, says 'Hey, why should I? I've got as much right to be here as he has!' The impulses to fight or run away are therefore at war with each other. Sometimes we stand our ground, sometimes we give in. And often we do neither, it appears, entirely full-heartedly.

It is only a theory, but it may help to account for why people, in times of war, may feel torn in two, the desire for a quiet life (reptilian submission) and the desire for freedom (our front brain's recognition of justice and injustice) being at war within our own bodies. War is being waged on the inside as well as on the out.

Such was the case, it seems, during the first great war for which we have a poetic account – the war between the Greeks and the Trojans. In Homer's *Iliad* (named after Ilium, another word for Troy) there is as much dissension within the rival armies as between them. And some of the main characters are at war with themselves, sometimes wanting to fight and sometimes leaving the battlefield in high dudgeon.

The war comes about, and is extended, because of women trouble: the problems the men are experiencing with some of the women. First, it's Helen. Paris, son of Priam, king of Troy, has abducted her from the house of her husband, Meneleus. Paris was a guest of Meneleus when he did the deed, so he has offended against one of the most fundamental laws: loyalty and protection between a host and a guest. (Law was simple at that time. The only other two interdictions were those that forbade blasphemy against the gods, and the shedding of kindred blood.)

Meneleus, king of Sparta, along with Agamemnon, king of Mycenae, Achilles with his Myrmidons and various other warriors, sail from Greece to Troy, where they camp for nine years beside their ships without being able to capture the city. A long time without the comforts of home.

But the Greeks, (who in *The Iliad* are called the Achaeans, the Argives and the Danaans, which sometimes can be confusing) had managed to loot a few towns around Troy, and captured two women. One, Chryseis (daughter of the priest of Apollo) was given to Agamemnon, the commander-in-chief, and the other, Briseis, to Achilles, the Argives' best warrior.

Trouble deepens when Chryseis has to be given back to her father, who has called on Apollo to send a plague on the Achaeans. Agamemnon, furious at having to give up 'his' woman, insists that Achilles hand over Briseis to fill the gap. After this, Achilles refuses to fight, and the Danaans are in danger of being trounced until Achilles' great friend Patroclus is killed and Achilles returns to the fray, killing Hector, the Trojans' own best warrior.

In his grief and fury, Achilles has the body of Hector dragged around his friend's grave every day, until Priam, Hector's father, comes to him at night with a ransom, begging for his son's body back. Achilles gives in to Priam's own grief. In the secrecy of the night, the two men are united in their mourning, and *The Iliad* closes with a truce for the funeral of Hector.

The Iliad is written in dactylic hexameters: ONE two three, ONE two three, ONE two three – a strong beat followed by two weak beats. There are six of these in every line. Coming in on a stressed beat gives a lot of energy to a line, causing it to gallop along, rather than walking soberly as the iamb does.

To remember how the dactyl works, think of a finger ('dactyl' means finger). It has one long joint and two short ones, doesn't it? That's why the Greeks called it that. They composed in long and short syllables, rather than strong and weak beats, as we do. We use their names for metre, even though we compose in strong and weak beats, the stressed and unstressed syllables we inherited from the tribes who invaded us from northern Europe during what we rather quaintly call the Dark Ages, which were in fact the time of some of our most stunning poetry. Invasion and warfare can bring in new forms of poetry, too. It's not all raping and pillaging.

But I don't want to be concerned too much with metre here. What I'm interested in is getting inside some of the characters, especially the more horrid ones, to try to get behind their monstrosity and see from where it arises.

Let's begin with Agamemnon himself, commander-in-chief of the Greek forces, and incredibly ruthless, greedy and selfish: a perfect model for a twenty-first century dictator. He goes so far in his prideful arrogance that he commits the sin of *hubris*, which means overstepping the bounds, claiming for himself what should only belong to the gods. For this the gods have to impose *dike*, which means a re-establishing of order, by allowing him to be brutally murdered by his wife and his wife's lover.

Agamemnon begins by slaughtering his own daughter, Iphigenia, in order to get a fair wind so his ships can sail to Troy. Here we have the shedding of kindred blood, one of the three major crimes, so we know, even before the war starts, that there is big trouble in store for him.

But can you hear his rationale? 'What else could I do? The soothsayer said we'd never get there without the sacrifice. Men have to do terrible things in order to win. I am a soldier, after all.'

Then he takes Chryseis, daughter of one of Apollo's priests. ('She's mine, as war booty. Only the brave deserve the fair, and who is braver than I? I am the leader of the Danaans.') When she returns to her father, he takes Briseis away from Achilles, his best soldier. ('Women are all the same. He can always find another. But I must have the pick of the bunch. And all women, and all men, even Achilles, must yield to me.')

When the Greeks have won, Agamemnon claims Cassandra, the Trojan prophetess and daughter of Priam, as his prize, even though she warns him that they will both be murdered when he returns to Mycenae and Clytemnestra, his wife. ('Stupid woman. Why should my own wife murder me? She's ranting, mad. Sexy though. I don't mind having her in my bed.')

Agamemnon's final crime, upon his return to his palace, is to walk on the purple carpet Clytemnestra has laid down for him. Purple is the gods' colour: he is arrogating to himself a privilege of the gods. The carpet leads to his bath, and it is here that Clytemnestra and Aegisthus, her lover, murder him, having made him helpless beforehand by helping him into a bathrobe that is in effect a straitjacket.

Here is your first war poem. Imagine yourself as Agamemnon. You have just been murdered, and you are utterly at a loss. Why has Clytemnestra done this? Haven't you been away for ten years doing the honourable thing, avenging the honour of her sister (Helen and Clytemnestra are twins)? Haven't you fought bravely and returned the victor, bringing with you some of the spoils of Troy?

Write a dramatic monologue, a poem from Agamemnon's point of view, where you express what he thinks about the whole business, but in a way that also reveals him for what he is. You don't need to worry about how to do this: just let him explain to the reader what he's done, and he'll condemn himself out of his own mouth. When a character does this in a poem, a play or a novel (revealing things to the reader that they are not aware of themselves), it is called 'dramatic irony'.

Be careful not to allow any of your own moral judgments to creep into the poem. Your task here is to become Agamemnon, horrible as he is, so that the reader can begin to understand his monstrosity, rather than simply condemning him. All dictators and mass-murderers have ample reason for what they do. If you look into the lives of any of them, as psychoanalysts and psycho-historians have done, you will find the origins of their love of cruelty. And you will find yourself weeping, as much for the dictator as for those he tyrannized over. The tragedy belongs to the tyrant as well as to the victims.

Think of yourself as the detective who has to enter into the mind of the murderer, to mentally become the murderer, in order to catch him.

Now sit down and write the first draft of your poem.

Then, as you did before, read it over coolly and without judgment, and put it away in your war chest.

PRETEXTS FOR WAR

And what of Helen, the supposed reason for all this palaver? When she understands the extent of the destruction, she wants to give up her life with

Paris, and says as much to Aphrodite. ('I refuse to go and share his bed again –
I should never hear the end of it. There is not a woman in Troy who would not
curse me if I did. I have enough to bear already.')

But there are greater forces at work than Helen's own willpower. The
Olympian gods and goddesses have sided variously with the Greeks and
Trojans, so the battle is as much between invisible forces as between two
human armies. Each major god or goddess has a favourite (Paris is Aphrodite's
favourite; Odysseus of the nimble wits is favoured by Athene) and they are
all determined to save the one they love the most. And although the abduction
of Helen may have been the pretext for the siege of Troy, once it has begun
she watches helplessly as the human and inhuman forces play themselves
out.

What would it be like to be Helen, the woman with the beautiful body who is
fought over? Someone with the power to start a war but without the power to
stop it? Or, analogously, what would it be like to be anything that people fight
over? What would it be like to be oil, for example, or land, or any of the
'commodities' deemed precious enough for men to go to war over?

Put yourself in the position of the precious object, and imagine the feelings
and voice of one of the pretexts for war. What would happen if one of the sides
had to do without the thing they want? If the West had gone without some of
its oil, for example, rather than beginning the Gulf War in 1991? What might
the oil have had to say about it? Or what might the land of North America have
wanted to say when the white settlers were claiming it as part of their manifest
destiny? What might it feel like to be occupied by one kind of people (nomadic,
warriors, buffalo-hunters, animists) and then by another, quite different kind
(farmers, miners, settled city-dwellers, monotheists)? One kind who believed
that the land contained its own spirit, and another who believed that it was
theirs to do as they liked with?

Put yourself into the mind and body of the pretext for war, and write what
they might have to say about it.

Read your draft, then put it away.

THE COMMENTATORS

There are two other tantalizing details in *The Iliad* that I would like you to
explore in your poems. The first is a note at the end of E.V. Rieu's translation
that says:

> one of our manuscripts contains a remark by an annotator to the effect
> that certain authorities substituted for the last line the words: 'Such were
> the funeral rites of Hector. And now came an Amazon ...'

The last line of Rieu's translation is

> Such were the funeral rites of Hector, tamer of horses.

So it looks as though some scholars had the poem continuing, and that the Amazon here was Queen Penthesilia, who came to help Priam, fought Achilles, and was killed by him.

What do you think the Amazon queen would have said to herself when she saw the graves of Hector and Patroclus, the bodies still unburied around the city walls, the city of Troy itself, deteriorating daily as its customary trade was cut off by the siege, and the family of Priam, divided against itself as Paris, its youngest son, harbours a queen whose presence in Troy caused the whole sorry business in the first place?

Remember that the Amazons were female warriors. They were called barbarians by the Greeks, and thought to live by the Black Sea. It may be that they were a myth themselves, invented by the Greeks for their own purposes. They were thought to expose boy children on the mountainsides and bring up their girls to be warriors, cutting off one of their breasts so they could draw the bow more effectively. In battle, although they were very brave and skilful, they were believed to always lose, in the end, to the Greeks. In fact, the graves of large-boned women buried with armour have been discovered near the Black Sea, so perhaps they did exist after all.

The Amazons lived by fighting, so they wouldn't be surprised by slaughter. But slaughter on this scale, and all for one stolen queen? What would the Queen of the Amazons say to this?

Begin your poem 'And now there came an Amazon'.

When you have written the first draft, put it away.

The second detail, along similar lines, concerns Zeus himself. Sitting on Mount Ida, he got tired, sometimes, of watching the endless battle, so he turned 'his shining eyes into the distance' where he could see 'the Abii, the most law-abiding folk on earth'. So somewhere in Homer's embattled world there lived another kind of people, a people who had fashioned their lives so they did not have to fight one another.

What would their lives be like? Utopian or dystopian? Would they be ruled by love or by fear? Let your imagination range over the possibilities available for a people who have gone beyond warfare.

Call your poem 'Zeus turned his shining eyes into the distance' and write your first draft of it now.

These last two poems will help you to see warfare through the eyes of outsiders who construct their lives in different ways, and so endow warfare with a patina of strangeness, as the reader sees it through new eyes, as if for the first time. Looking at a war that is thought to have been first written about in 1200BCE will also do this: the long view brings humour and balance.

Before we leave *The Iliad*, I want us to consider the extraordinary scene very near the end, when King Priam, with the magical aid of Hermes, comes to Achilles' tent to plead for the body of his son Hector, whom Achilles has killed, so he can give him the proper funeral rites. The two men do not meet as enemies, but as two human beings who have lost most of those they love.

Priam reminds Achilles of his own father, whom he has had to leave in order to pursue this war. He says to Achilles:

> ... fear the gods, and be merciful to me, remembering your own father,
> though I am even more entitled to compassion, since I have brought
> myself to do a thing that no one else on earth has done – I have raised to
> my lips the hand of the man who killed my son.

And Achilles agrees to return Hector's body to him. Then Achilles orders his men to slaughter a sheep and they sit down and eat a good meal together.

Consider it: two men whose armies have faced each other for nine years. Achilles has killed Priam's eldest son, and Paris will soon kill the ill-starred Achilles, though Achilles' death is not included in *The Iliad* itself. Death lies all around them, but in the little space of Achilles' tent they make their own temporary peace, man to man, father to son. Priam makes Achilles think of his own father Peleus, and Achilles, in his soldierly manliness, reminds Priam of the beauty of his own dead son. They each merge into the one that the other has lost, and in doing this they are no longer the other's enemy, but their best beloved. War merges into truce, which merges into love.

There may be moments in every war when all becomes still, stunned into recognition, and both sides silently count their losses, considering perhaps whether the enemy, with sons and fathers just like their own, is really, in essence, an enemy at all. I experienced a moment like this in Atocha Station in Madrid, after the terrorist attack of 11 March 2004. The station was filled with red candles, incense filled the air and people moved around quietly, looking at the photographs of the dead and the signs of *Paz* (Peace) that were hung around the concourse. And I wondered what it would be like if a young man who had participated in the attack should come to the station and see the silent human grief, and whether the war could carry on if we really knew what we were doing to one another.

When Priam faces Achilles and they take the measure of each other's grief, the war has to cease, if only for a while. If my imaginary young man, likewise, came to Atocha Station, saw and experienced the depth of emotion, and an old man, the father of one of those killed, embraced him as a fellow-sufferer – what would have been the effect?

I want you to bring this situation into yourself now as the subject of your poem. Two enemies meet. Perhaps one of them doesn't know that they are enemies, or perhaps they both do. The line I want you to use as a working title, to start off your thoughts, is Priam's 'I have raised to my lips the hand of the man who killed my son', with all its evocations both of reconciliation and betrayal. In reconciling with one's enemy, is one betraying one's own dead? Consider these things as you write the draft of your poem.

And when you have written it, put it away until later.

THE COLD WAR

The Trojan War was a very hot war: lots of hand-to-hand fighting, the living soldiers in the constant presence of the dead, the immediacy of siege-warfare. But after the Second World War, thousands of years later, the Western world entered into a time of ice. Winston Churchill said that until the world was ruled by love it would have to be held in the chains of fear – and this is in fact what happened. The Soviet Union and the USA both possessed weapons of mass destruction, and neither used them for fear of reprisals. They hardly communicated with each other, digging ever deeper and deeper into their isolation.

The philosopher Theodore Adorno said 'After Auschwitz, no poetry is possible.' Yet the poets of what was the Eastern bloc, born just after the war into a time of secrecy and persecution, have showed us the kind of poetry that can emerge after the killing fields, when the difficult truce between East and West involved totalitarian rule by the Communist Party in many countries, and a manufactured fear of communism in the West.

The poet and playwright Bertolt Brecht wrote:

In the dark times, will there also be singing?
Yes, there will be singing about the dark times.

The post-war generation of poets in Eastern Europe wrote poetry that shows us exactly what this means.

Ioana Craciunescu is a Romanian poet, born in 1950, who is also an actress, working in cabaret, theatre and film. I would like you to take a look at two of her poems.

Abundance in Suffering

Without heads, without guts, with hearts beating
on a rubbish heap, each one
peeling off its skin in tubs of salt,
the eels are still thrashing about.

The tear sniffs out the eye.

The eye is the water in which I see them swimming,
twisting about, eels turning the grass
blood-red.

Knives are an extension of our caresses;
love is a remembering of this butchery.

City Without a Biography

In this city
the mute make declarations of love to each other
in different words.

In shop windows
on Persian carpets, faded women
learn Persian.

Under gas masks we hold in our teeth
wallets of papers
(the photo of mud-brick houses
in the fog)

Over my body runs an otter – your mouth
lost in the night.

In both poems there is an experience of tremendous suffering – and yet within the suffering there is also love.

What do you think the eels signify in the first poem? To me they are a metaphor for suffering, but also for not being able to give up. The poet sees them, and yet they are also part of herself ('The eye is the water in which I see them swimming'). She seems to know that she is part of the blood-letting ('Knives are an extension of our caresses') – as she is also a part of the possible recovery ('love is a remembering of this butchery'). Remembering involves putting things back together that have been broken or fragmented. This is also the task of poetry.

In the second poem, people try to hold on to things and to hold on to love in a city that has lost its biography, lost its history. This also involves a wiping-out of memory. Language seems to have been taken away, yet 'the mute make declarations of love to each other.' People even learn another language, Persian (traditionally, the language of love) in order to get away from being mute. And the beloved becomes part of the natural world ('Over my body runs an otter – your mouth /lost in the night').

In both poems, love is pitched against suffering. As if the armies of love had laid siege to the city of suffering. And although they are both bleak poems, there is nothing passive about them, no blaming of others (the Party or the Secret Police), however obliquely, for what is going on. The poet admits her own part in it, and her own part, too, in ending the destruction.

Again we see the proximity of love and hate, desire and destruction, that we encountered in some of the love poems. Consider again why and how these two feelings, that we imagine to be at opposite ends of the spectrum, should keep coming together.

I am writing this chapter in Galicia, in northern Spain, near to where General Franco was born. After his army had beaten the Republican forces, Franco held Spain under his tyranny for almost forty years. In the fishing village where I stay, I am told of people being beaten to death, or shot, for the slightest infringement of Franco's laws. Or killed at whim, simply because his henchmen felt like it. If parents were at all left-wing, their children could be taken away from them and put in orphanages until good fascist parents were found. Bodies are still being discovered in shallow graves by the roadsides. All this in Spain (not Albania, not the Congo), and recently.

So how is tyranny endured, by the people who cannot escape it? There may be a mass exodus, of people who have somewhere to go or are willing to leave everything behind. But most of the population have to stay. What is it like, do you think, for them?

Your next poem will explore the experience of tyranny. You may well know something about it already, even if you haven't lived under a tyrannous political regime. The bullying teacher, the parent with irrational rages, the cruel sibling, all these teach us what it's like to have freedom and justice taken away from us.

Write down the characteristics of tyranny. What does it look like, taste like, smell like, sound like? How does it feel in your skin? And are you yourself, in any way, a part of it, as Craciunescu acknowledges herself to be in 'Abundance in suffering'? If you are, what might you do to stop being part of the problem, to become a part of the recovery? How have you tyrannized over yourself, and how can you break the bonds, let go of the police state inside? There is a theory that we get the governments we deserve, that if there is tyranny, at some level we have consented to it. If that is true, how can we break the consent?

Let the previous sentence be the theme of your poem. Imagine everything that tyranny is, and then imagine the sorts of actions, thoughts, work, leisure, paintings, music, poems, that would begin to see an end to it, make it impossible for it to thrive any longer. Tyrants are particularly keen to control the work of artists, in case they undermine the state in an encoded way in their work, and many artists have suffered or died because they could not give up the practice of freedom that their art required. On the other hand, the poet Shelley claimed that the poets are the unacknowledged legislators of society, and it does seem, from what we read of the Russian poets, for example, that it was their vision that came to pass, rather than the vision of Stalin, who tried to destroy them.

Now write the first draft of your poem.

When it is complete, read it and put it away. Shake yourself all over to free yourself from the experience of tyranny, and take the rest of the day off from writing, in order to fully enjoy the freedoms you might normally take for granted. The art of slipping into someone else's skin is an essential part of being a writer, but there is a cost, because some experiences, like the one you've just been through, can be damaging if you stay inside them for too long. The mind, body and heart are damaged by tyranny. So shake yourself loose from it now, and enjoy the life you have. It might even seem so astonishing to you (like the sudden availability of bananas after the Second World War) that you want to write a poem about it. But rest first.

THE BLACK HUMOUR OF TYRANNY

Humour can be a brilliant, although also dangerous, weapon against tyranny. The Polish poet Tomasz Jastrun uses it savagely in some of his poems. Born in 1950, he jointed the Gdansk shipyard workers during the 1980 August strikes, and went into hiding when martial law was declared. He was arrested in 1982 and interned. Two volumes of his poetry were brought out in *samizdat*, the secretly-printed and distributed government-banned literature that circulated during the times of tyranny. So he himself is an example of a poet who was prepared to risk a great deal in order to continue with his commitment to authenticity. Take a look at this poem, which explores the ludicrous paranoia of tyranny, the way it tends to identify *anything* as dangerous.

Hat

This elderly gentleman
also takes walks in the Yard
But his hat clashes
with the barbed wire
and the bars muzzling the windows
as though they were afraid we might bite through
This man with a hat
is here because he sought
to overthrow the government by force
and violate our treaties.

Sixty years old
his hands furrowed like the earth
of pre-war Europe
and a very dangerous hat
on his head.

Presumably the elderly gentleman has been imprisoned for something other than wearing a dangerous-looking hat, yet the hat is a symbol of his threat to the state, a symbol that indicates how ridiculous and superficial is the nature of his offence against authority.

In Shakespeare's *Henry VI*, a man is hanged for 'whistling treason' – whistling a song that involved criticism or rebellion against civil authority. Salmun Rushdie had to go into hiding for years for writing a book which was deemed to have criticized the prophet Mahommed. The French government has decided that Moslem girls wearing headscarves to school is a threat to the secularity of the state, and has passed a law forbidding them to do so. The Puritans destroyed all the paintings on English church walls because they believed them to be idolatrous. A song, a book, a headscarf, church paintings – how many more things can you think of that have been destroyed or banned because of the sensitivities of a particular government? The Irish and Welsh languages, for example, had to go underground because the English occupying forces wanted to know what was being said, and so prevented their being taught in schools. What else?

What, in your own life, do you see as a symbol of your own freedom and your own individuality? Is it an object, an activity, a custom, or something else? Now imagine yourself, like the elderly man in the hat, being targeted for using it or doing it. How would you try to protect this aspect of yourself? To what lengths would you go to continue with it?

When you write your poem, let your voice be quiet and unassuming, as Jastrun's is in 'Hat'. You want the import of what you say to creep up on your reader slowly, so that the full ludicrousness of the ban dawns gradually, as the poem goes along.

Now write the poem.

When you've written the first draft, put it away in your war chest and consider the next question discussed below.

THE CHILDREN OF TYRANNY

What is it like for the next generation, for those actually born into tyranny? Brecht, who left Germany for America before the Second Word War, wrote a very moving poem called 'To those who come later,' where he asks forgiveness of the next generation because his own, in struggling against oppression, have themselves been damaged by it. His poem says 'Hatred, even of meanness/distorts the features.' We can imagine the children looking at their parents and wondering why their faces and bodies are disfigured by the tics and tribulations that signify what they have been through.

William Blake saw these signs on the bodies of the people of London. Walking through the city, he wrote:

> I walk thro' every charter'd street
> Near where the charter'd Thames does flow
> And mark on every face I meet
> Marks of weakness, marks of woe.

Oppression is written on the body, and the children, whose minds and bodies preserve for a while the freedom and freshness that is their birthright, may look at their parents and wonder how they have come to this.

Consider another poem by Tomasz Jastrun, of whom the editor Michael March (in *Child of Europe – A New Anthology of European Poetry*, Penguin

Books, from which I have quoted these poems) has said: 'Though he would deny the charge, he is the finest poet of his generation.'

Fruit

Even love
Can be torn away
Like dressing
Off the great wound of the face

Even that wound
Can be torn away

The scream remains

And even it
Can breed
Wild fruit

Our hungry children
Reach

What does the poem say to you?

To me, it is trying to discover if anything lies behind love. If love is not available, or has run out or been burned away, is there something else that lies behind it? Behind the bandages of love lies the wound of the face, and behind that lies the scream, which has its own fertility and breeds 'wild fruit' which the children, hungry as they are, reach for.

My daughter had a schoolfriend whose father had been imprisoned in Chile under Pinochet. The father would take his food and his cigarettes and eat and smoke in the toilet. He had had his food stolen from him so often that the toilet seemed the only place of safety. That was his tragedy. But there was also the tragedy of his daughter, who couldn't sit, relaxed with her father, while they ate a meal together. That most basic sociability had been destroyed.

What kind of children, do you think, would be born under tyranny? Is there a natural urge towards freedom, so the children would continue the struggle of their parents? Or might the children consider their parents' struggle futile, a waste of time, and turn their attention to what pleasures there might be in the present? Or would they seek to escape from present reality into some mind-altered state?

How would they regard their parents? Even if the parents believe that they have the government they deserve, do their children deserve it? What choice did they have, and what kind of feelings might that knowledge generate? Fury? Resentment? Or a shrugging disaffection, a refusal to engage at any level?

Consider these questions, and any others that might come to you, and then put yourself in a position between the parent and the child. What is happening? Write it down. Again, let your voice be calm and quiet, because there is immense drama here. The drama will emerge far more effectively in your poem if it is told calmly. Powerful feelings come over best in the still small voice that comes after the storms and the earthquakes.

Now write your poem.

And again, once you've written it, put it away and give yourself some time off. This work that writers do, where you allow yourself, for a time, to become someone else, is tiring, even though it is necessary. Come back to your own life gently, appreciating anew, again, the freedoms you have, and becoming more aware too, perhaps, of the subtle restrictions you live under.

COMMITTED POETRY

The poets of Eastern Europe had no choice about engaging in the struggle for greater tolerance and freedom, but in the West, since the end of the nineteenth century, there has existed a trend that sets the artist and poet outside society, in an attitude of disaffection and alienation. There have been good reasons for this, perhaps the greatest of which is the industrial revolution, which removed people from their heartlands and harnessed them to machines. This happened in my own family, whose members bore the scars, physical and mental, of the long hours of factory work with its noise, harsh discipline and alienated labour.

But a position of alienation and removal isn't much use for a poet if your country is fighting a war that you passionately oppose, and you want to use your poetry as part of the struggle towards peace. Holding yourself aloof from your society might work in easier times, but in times of war the poets have always had a crucial part to play, whether as troubadours offering courage, in song, to the troops, or as a choir of opposition, singing that there is another way, if only we will look for it.

During the First World War, Wilfred Owen, and during the Gulf War, Tony Harrison, wrote poems that gazed so far into the conflict that they seemed to enter the minds of those who were called the enemy. Owen's 'Strange Meeting' and Harrison's 'A Cold Coming' both imagine a dead enemy speaking to them, giving them truths beyond the understanding of war, and both write their poem, interestingly, in rhyming couplets, as though the harmony of rhyme might have something to say to the disharmony of destruction.

Owen's 'Strange Meeting' has a soldier meeting the enemy he killed the previous day in a spiritual no-man's land that could be the afterlife. Like Harrison, Owen experiences the privilege (which, in real life, could only happen with difficulty) of hearing the longings of the soldier from the other side. Here is a portion of the poem:

'Strange friend,' I said, 'here is no cause to mourn.'
'None,' said that other, 'save the undone years,
The hopelessness. Whatever hope is yours,
Was my life also; I went hunting wild
After the wildest beauty in the world,
Which lies not calm in eyes, or braided hair
But mocks the steady running of the hour,
And if it grieves, grieves richlier than here ...

I would have poured my spirit without stint
But not through wounds; not on the cess of war.
Foreheads of men have bled where no wounds were.
I am the enemy you killed, my friend.
I knew you in this dark; for so you frowned
Yesterday through me as you jabbed and killed.
I parried; but my hands were loath and cold.
Let us sleep now ...

The trusty iamb limps its way through this poem, too, giving weight and measure to feelings that might otherwise lift the poem too high in their intensity. Owen is using the iamb here to hold the poem down, to ground it in some terrain the reader can recognize, even though he is actually taking us into hell. When he reaches the famous line, 'I am the enemy you killed, my friend,' the iamb is dropped and he changes gear, using the more energetic dactyl (one hard, followed by two soft beats) to give emphasis and cause the reader to pause and read it again. We may not know why we pause, and indeed Owen may not have known consciously that he was shifting the metre, but nevertheless it is the metrical change that accounts, to some degree, for the power of this line.

I would also like to draw your attention to these lines:

for so you frowned
Yesterday through me as you jabbed and killed.
I parried; but my hands were loath and cold.
Let us sleep now ...

What do you think 'frowned ... through me' means? And why were the enemy's hands 'loath and cold' when he tried to strike back?

For me, Owen is pointing to an identification between the two men. One frowning through the other could mean that the frown pierced through the so-called enemy, or that the enemy frowned on behalf of the narrator of the poem. Either way, there is a merging, a coming-together. And the fact that his hands were 'loath and cold' when he came to strike back, indicates an unwillingness to kill the man who, though his enemy, is nevertheless, essentially, his friend. The poet Jon Silkin has suggested that the enemy is loath to kill because 'to do so would have entailed the self-infliction of a psychic wound'. And this, perhaps, takes us to the heart of darkness of warfare: that in killing our enemies we are in fact killing a part of ourselves.

It is this identification that Tony Harrison takes on in 'A Cold Coming'. Here, the two men are not in any way interchangeable, though: it's first world and third world. The Iraqi soldier Harrison causes to speak is the one caught on the front pages in that blood-chilling picture of the Iraqi retreat to Baghdad. The dead soldier who speaks knows that his life-chances are very different from those of the US soldiers:

> On Saddam's pay we can't afford
> to go and get our semen stored.
>
> Sad to say that such high tech's
> uncommon here. We're stuck with sex.

Even if they get killed, the US Marines 'who banked their sperm before the battle' can still have children, still send their genes down to the next generation, whereas for the Iraqi soldier, once he's gone, he's gone.

Harrison's ghostly soldier has none of the high yearnings of Owen's. Harrison imagines him a man bound by the prejudices of his time, quite simply mightily fed up that he's been killed, and refusing any noble feelings about brotherly love:

> Pretend I've got the imagination
> to see the world beyond one nation.
>
> That's your job, poet, to pretend
> I want my foe to be my friend.
>
> It's easier to find such words
> for this dumb mask like baked dogturds.
>
> So lie and say the charred man smiled
> to see the soldier hug his child.
>
> This gaping rictus once made glad
> a few old hearts back in Baghdad,
>
> hearts growing older by the minute
> as each truck comes without me in it.
>
> I've met you though, and had my say
> which you've got taped. Now go away.

It's a very different mood from Owen's, isn't it? Dour, sour, recalcitrant, refusing the possibility of forgiveness or reconciliation. Harrison fathoms some of the hatred and envy that a third world 'enemy soldier' must feel, a hatred the West has been forced to recognize since its further escapades in Iraq.

Think yourself, now, into the position of a soldier. Suddenly, there before you, is a man or woman you've been trained to see as your enemy. What do they look like? What is the expression of their face? And how do you yourself feel inside? What's happening in your chest, and in your guts? Write all this down.

What do you say to each other? Do you say anything, or do you just look, and think?

What is the outcome? Do you kill them, or they you? Or does something else supervene? And if you don't kill them, how do you return to your regiment? Or, like Owen's soldiers, are you beyond the grave when you have your strange meeting?

You may find that you want to spend some time sitting with this problem before you broach it in a poem. Take as long as you like. If you plant the questions in your mind, sometimes they are answered in your dreams or in thoughts that come to you while you are doing something else.

For this poem, I'd like you to try writing an elegy. This form, for the Greeks and Romans, meant any poem written in alternating hexameter and pentameter lines (six metrical feet followed by five) which they called the elegiac metre. So one line should have twelve syllables, or six stresses to a line, and the next should have ten syllables, or five stresses. And, if you want to capture the harmony-within-conflict of Owen's and Harrison's poems, you can also make them rhyme. If you do this, remember that you don't have to use the full rhymes of Harrison's poem all the time (pretend/friend, words/dogturds, smiled/child, glad/Baghdad). The half-rhymes of Owen's poem can be even more effective (war/were, friend/frowned, killed/cold) in giving the reader a feeling of harmony without the danger of glibness that a perfect rhyme can bring. (Full rhymes are sometimes called perfect rhymes or true rhymes, and half rhymes can also be called imperfect rhymes, slant rhymes, near rhymes or pararhymes.)

And your poem needn't stick to end-rhymes, either (where the rhyme comes at the end of the line): rhymes within the lines, called internal rhymes, which don't smack the reader in the face, but establish themselves slowly, can give a sense of hidden harmony within the turbulence and grief of the poem.

The term 'elegy', as well as describing the metre, also means a poem that explores questions of change and loss, often including complaints about love. As we were saying before, the two often seem to come together.

Now sit down and write the first draft of your poem.

Read it, and put it away.

Poets are, by the nature of their interests and the nature of artistic fabrication, singularly ill-equipped to understand politics or economics ...

The poet cannot understand the function of money in modern society because for him there is no relation between subjective value and market value; he may be paid ten pounds for a poem which he believes is very good and took him months to write, and a hundred pounds for a piece of journalism which costs him but a day's work ...

All poets adore explosions, thunderstorms, tornadoes, conflagrations, ruins, scenes of spectacular carnage. The poetic imagination is not at all a desirable quality in a statesman.

In a war or a revolution, a poet may do very well as a guerrilla fighter or a spy, but it is unlikely that he will make a good regular soldier, or, in peace time, a conscientious member of a parliamentary committee.

W.H. Auden, 'The Poet and the City', in *The Dyer's Hand* (Random House, 1962)

POEMS OF RESISTANCE

Then there are the poems that valiantly resist the invasions of outside imperial forces, or sing in praise of the struggle for independence and self-determination. Many beautiful poems of this kind have emerged out of Central America, which has suffered immensely at the hands of its powerful northern neighbour. I've chosen two which I think give a sense of the work and risk involved in the work of resistance. The first is by Vidaluz Meneses, who was born in Nicaragua and eventually took over the management of the Library and Archives Department at the Nicaraguan Ministry of Culture.

Minimum Homage

With production at an all-time low
Without sufficient typewriters or
even desks,
we are taking up the challenge
of the second phase of your work, Carlos,
and it reminds me of when you took to the mountains with a few
    comrades, fewer arms
and a banner.

The Carlos referred to in the poem is Carlos Fonseca, who was the military commander of the first Sandinista National Liberation Front, killed in 1976. And the strength of the poem, I think, emerges out of 'and it reminds me of ...' where the poet compares the work she herself is doing with the more obvious warriorship of Carlos Fonseca. There are more ways of bringing about a revolution, she seems to be saying, than just fighting. The fighting may come first, and the martyrdoms, but the second, difficult phase of building a free nation, is equally important. If the second phase doesn't succeed, then the fighting was in vain.

The second poem is by Ana Maria Rodas, from Guatamala. Born in 1944, she became a journalist, returned to night school in 1981 and then became a lecturer at San Carlos University.

Now I Know

Now I know
I'll never be other than one
of love's guerrillas.
I find my place somewhere
roughly on the erotic left wing.

Loosing bullet after bullet
at the system
Losing strength and time
in preaching my nocturnal gospel

Perhaps I'll end up like that other madman
gunned down in the sierra

But since my struggle
is of no political consequence to men,
my journal will never seek a publisher
nor will my photograph
adorn their hoardings.

Translated by Amanda Hopkinson, from Lovers and Comrades – Women's Resistance Poetry from Central America *(Women's Press, UK, 1989)*

The 'other madman' of the poem is Che Guevara, who was killed in Bolivia in 1967. The poet identifies with him, because she herself is conducting a secret war, one that is invisible politically, but which nevertheless may have consequences involving the freeing of erotic desire from restrictions and conventions.

There is the implication here, too, that Che's death would have been in vain unless the relations of daily life are also able to change. We are back to the terrain of the love poems, where adult sexual love can only be completely fulfilled after certain political, social and cultural changes have come about: people can only love one another as equals after their society has reached a certain level of development.

Now imagine yourself as someone whose society has experienced a huge political upheaval, perhaps brought about by armed uprising. You have already sacrificed a great deal, and it's time now to begin to build the kind of society you want. What kind of society *do* you want? What are the things worth fighting for? Which changes are dearest to your heart? This is the other side of your poems about tyranny, where you allow yourself to imagine the characteristics of daily life in the society you've already suffered for.

What will life be like? Will everyone have a car and a television, or will you get rid of these things? Will people live in houses? How will they work? How spend their leisure time? Think of all the attributes of what you believe to be the good life, the life more abundant, and write them down.

How will people take to these new conditions, do you think? Will they rejoice and make the most of them, or find more reasons to be dissatisfied? Can people bear to be happy, or will they have to ruin things all over again? If they do, what will you do with the malcontents?

Now write your poem. Read it, and put it away.

A SINGLE THOUGHT

There are some poems, and some songs, that are so totally focussed, and speak so directly to the events of a certain time, that they have a deep and immediate impact on the citizens of a country. They make things happen. It can be what a poem or a song does for people's spirits that can tip a society one way or the other.

The French poet Paul Eluard wrote a poem called 'A Single Thought' which he placed first in his collection *Poetry and Truth*, published secretly in occupied France in 1942. The title of the poem was later changed to 'Liberty,' and under this title it was parachuted into France by the British Royal Air Force, in containers aimed at the French Resistance who were hiding out in the countryside. Here is a version of it in English.

Liberty

On my schoolbooks
On my desk and on the trees
On the sand and on the snow
I write your name

On all the pages I have read
On all the blank pages
Stone blood paper or ash
I write your name ...

On my greedy, tender dog
On his pricked-up ears
On his clumsy paw
I write your name ...

On health which has returned
On the risk which has disappeared
On the hope without memory
I write your name

And by the power of one word
I begin my life again
I was born to know you
To name you

Liberty.

The entire poem is in fact four times longer than this. Can you imagine the impact of it, appearing out of the sky, upon Resistance fighters hiding in caves in the Auvergne? Just one word can be all it takes, sometimes, to give courage to someone who's cold and hungry and whose spirits are low. And one word, implied, hinted at, then bursting out at the end of the poem must have the effect of saying it again and again, at first softly, under the breath, and then with more and more confidence and force, until the word and the desires that surround it seem to cause the air to resonate with its sound and its requirements.

Poems and songs do have an effect in the world. Think of the song 'Feed the World' and the role it played in raising money to ease the famine in Ethiopia. Think of the mantra that Mahatma Gandhi chanted every day of his life (Om Sri Rama Jaya Rama, Jaya Jaya Rama), a spiritual practice that undoubtedly helped him to win independence for his country, and which was on his lips even as he was murdered.

Now think of the word, or words, that are more precious to you than all the rest. Which word, or words, can you not live without? Write them down. What do they make you think of? Which objects, images, metaphors, smells, textures, tastes, come into your mind as you say these words? Write them down. Which rhythms come to you? Do your words have a tune? Are they loud or soft, or does their dynamic change? What is the *timbre* of these words – their quality of sound? What is their tempo – are they fast or slow? Note all these things down.

Imagine that your poem, like Eluard's, is going to be dropped into enemy territory to inspire and encourage the forces of resistance. How will you write your words in a way that will lift their spirits? Imagine how they will feel when they read it. And imagine it falling into enemy hands. How will it make your enemy feel?

Now write your poem. You might like to write it in four-line unrhyming stanzas, as Eluard did, or use rhyming couplets again, as you did in your last poem. Or perhaps the rhythms and requirements of everyday speech are precious to you here, so you need to write in free verse. Free verse for a poem about freedom, free from the trammels of regular rhythm and rhyme. You choose.

I think there is a 'fluid' as well as a 'solid' content, that some poems may have a form as a tree has form, some as water poured into a vase. That most symmetrical forms have certain uses. That a vast number of subjects cannot be precisely, and therefore not properly rendered in symmetrical forms ...

I think one should write vers libre [free verse] only when one 'must', that is to say, only when the 'thing' builds up a rhythm more beautiful than that of set metres, or more real, more a part of the emotion of the 'thing', more germane, intimate, interpretative than the measure of regular accentual verse; a rhythm which discontents one with set iambic or set anapaestic.

Ezra Pound, *The Literary Essays* (New Directions, USA, originally printed in *Poetry and Drama*, February 1912)

Reviewing Your Poems

Follow your normal routine of putting all your most recent poems away for a few days, and have a good rest. During this necessary fallow time, thoughts of war and peace will come to you, and your understanding of the place of harmony and conflict in our lives will deepen.

When you're ready to look at your poems again, I want you to read them with the aim of spotting anything that is sloppy or sentimental. Sentimentality is an emotion that's not real, that's put on for show, to manipulate the reader. According to the poet and psychoanalyst Valerie Sinason, it is a kind of sadism, where the writer works on the reader to produce an emotional effect, and then takes a voyeuristic pleasure in the reader's tears or vulnerability. You do want to produce strong feelings in your reader, but they must be feelings that you yourself share, that arise out of the situation you are describing in the poem.

If you find any lines or phrases, or even single words, that you've written only *for effect*, then strike them out and find words that simply and accurately represent the situation. The simplest words are often enough to make the reader feel the full impact of the situation you are exploring.

As always, you can feel the right words and the wrong words by the impact they have on your own body. The right words leave you feeling comfortable or, if they are saying something in a quite new way, exhilarated too. The wrong words, where you've gilded the lily or ventured into slush, will make you feel embarrassed at your over-cleverness. You know you are trying to mess with your reader's mind. (Your reader will know it too, and dislike you for it.) You can invent situations, places, characters and conflicts, but you must tell the simple truth about them, must be loyal to what Henry James called 'the truth of the imagination'.

5 Poems that Celebrate Cities

Cities are everywhere, just as Nature is everywhere. In 1850, a British census showed that, perhaps for the first time in human history, more people were living in towns than in the countryside. We tend to think of cities as phenomena that arise out of the industrial revolution: modern phenomena, that our ancestors didn't have to put up with. And yet recent archaeology has discovered very large settlements dating from the Iron Age. So perhaps the pull that people experience to live in large groups is also ancient, as is the desire to be alone, quiet and peaceful.

When I question people about their preferences for country or city, they often say that they find themselves caught between two worlds: when in the city, they long for the wide horizons of open land; and when in the country, they hunger for the conversations, the networks, and the entertainments of the city. They are never, quite, content in either place. It's the ambiguity of city life, its dangers and delights, that I want us to explore in this chapter. I want you to try to fathom some of our ambivalence towards cities, our feelings of love and hate towards them. And in plumbing these depths of emotion, discover the delights of what Keats called 'negative capability': the gift of holding contradictory feelings together.

In previous chapters we have explored the power of metaphor, of joining together what is with what is not, and so enhancing the lines of our language. When you are in a city, if you are anything like me, you may often feel that you do not know where you are, what is real and what isn't. Cities challenge our understanding of our world and ourselves, perhaps in a way that the country, with its regulated rhythms and cycles, does not. Cities, therefore, give us the chance to explore metaphor further, to see where it will take us.

William Blake, the poet whose 'Proverbs of Heaven and Hell' we looked at earlier, wrote a poem called 'London' which uses metaphor to represent the origins of some of the most destructive aspects of cities: the way they seem to drink the blood of their inhabitants and stand by silently while the worst things happen to them. Here it is:

London

I wander thro' each charter'd street
Near where the charter'd Thames does flow,
And mark in every face I meet
Marks of weakness, marks of woe.

In every cry of every Man,
In every Infant's cry of fear,
In every voice, in every ban,
The mind-forg'd manacles I hear.

How the Chimney-sweeper's cry
Every black'ning Church appalls;
And the hapless Soldier's sigh
Runs in blood down Palace walls.

But most thro' midnight streets I hear
How the youthful Harlot's curse
Blasts the new born Infant's tear
And blights with plagues the Marriage hearse.

The metaphors creep up slowly on us. At first it's just the signs of ownership: the streets and the river are chartered, staked out, owned. And the people's faces, too, bear the brand-marks of misery. Not literally, but metaphorically. If you look at photographs of children living on the streets of London in the nineteenth century (an excellent pamphlet, held at the Museum of London, is called *Spitalfields Nippers*) you will see from their faces that they look fifty years older than they actually are. London has aged them.

In the second verse the menace of the metaphor deepens: we hear the sound of manacles in every voice. The people of London, adults and children, bear witness, in the sounds of their voices, to the fact that their hands are chained. And these are not real chains. They are not really in prison. They are 'mind-forg'd manacles'. The chains that hold them exist only in their own minds. So the restrictions and prohibitions are those of belief and ideology. They aren't inevitable or imposed from above. They are of our own making. In all of Blake's poems you will find the theme that whatever world we inhabit, a heavenly world or a hellish world, we have made it ourselves.

The metaphor of the cry continues further in verse three. The cries spread everywhere. The chimney-sweepers, who died in their thousands of cancer of the scrotum because of the fires that were lit underneath them to force them up impossibly narrow chimneys, make a cry that appals the churches that are themselves blackened by London's myriad fires. The sigh of the soldier brings the blood of battlefields to the sumptuous surfaces of palaces. Cries cannot literally do these things, but within the world of the metaphor we can make these connections.

In the last verse Blake brings the literal and the metaphorical closer together: the curse of the young prostitute condemns to death the institution of marriage. An early version of his poem 'The Sick Rose' included the lines:

And dark secret love
Doth life destroy.

I think by this he meant that if we separate our loves into good and bad, virtuous and shameful, then we are condemned always to lead split lives: marriage and prostitution, the above-board with the illicit; and that the separation of our sexuality into two separate worlds condemns them both the ghostliness and unreality. The fact that the young harlot has to exist signals the destruction of marriage and the grief of the next generation ('the new born Infant's tear') both literally, in the passing-on of venereal diseases, and metaphorically, in the schizoid nature of our sexual pleasures.

It could be that whatever Blake had chosen – sights, sounds, smells, tastes, textures – would have led him deep into London's heart of darkness. Or it could equally be that there was no choice in the matter for him: the sounds just kept on until they forced him to write about them.

A book like this one suggests subjects to your conscious mind, which then sink down to the deeper levels of your being, where the poems and the need for poems are made. It is the sounds of the city I want you to concentrate on here. But these sounds will take you to the heart of the labyrinth of your own city, which may itself be a metaphor for your own mind.

THE CITY'S SOUNDS AND SILENCES

Go out into your own city now, or into a city near where you live, and find a place to sit. It can be indoors or outdoors (a park, a gallery, by a river or a canal), anywhere as long as you are in a public place.

Now just listen to the sounds, of traffic, birds, sirens, bells, people talking, and note down everything you can. Open your notebook flat and make your notes anywhere you want on the page. You will end up with a collage of city sounds sitting in a constellation on your lap.

Listen to the rhythm of your recorded sounds. Say them silently to yourself in your mind. You may have noticed that Blake, in 'London', often alternates the iambic metre with the trochaic: sometimes he begins a line with an unstressed beat, sometimes with a stressed. Even in the early nineteenth century, long before anyone had ever heard of jazz, Blake was creating a rhythmic syncopation when he wrote about London. You may find this syncopation (a ONE, a TWO, a ONE TWO THREE FOUR) emerging in your own mind.

Sprung Rhythm is the most natural of things. For (1) it is the rhythm of common speech and of written prose, when rhythm is perceived in them. (2) It is the rhythm of all but the most monotonously regular music, so that in the words of choruses and refrains and in songs written closely to music it arises. (3) It is found in nursery rhymes, weather saws, and so on; because, however these may have been once made in running rhythm [the trochaic foot: ONE two, ONE two, ONE two], the terminations having dropped off by the change of language, the stresses come together and so the rhythm is sprung. (4) It arises in common verse when reversed or counterpointed, for the same reason.

Gerard Manley Hopkins, from *Poems of Gerard Manley Hopkins* (Oxford University Press, 1948)

Or perhaps a sprung rhythm is emerging, where you have a certain number of stresses in each line, but no set number of syllables. Cities tend to overturn known patterns, to make chaos out of what we thought we knew and understood. Let them. Let the chaos and irregularity of the city invade your mind so that it can inform and penetrate your poem. Your poem needs to bear witness to the full complexity of the forces that go into its making. It will as long as you listen attentively to the sounds.

Now ask yourself where these sounds are taking you. Focus on each one in turn, close your eyes and follow the line of thread into the labyrinth. That police siren: what does it make you think of? Does it take you into the memory of a crime or an accident? Note it down. You hear church bells: what do they remind you of? You overhear workmen talking: where do the words take you? You see someone walking their dog: does it bring back childhood memories? This layering of the past over the present can create a powerful depth within your poems, rather like the effect of scumbling in painting, where a thin top layer of paint allows the spectator to see through to the images that lie beneath.

Or it may be that the present in all its fullness calls to you and insists on a primacy. The sounds don't remind you of anything: they are simply themselves, full of their own meaning and richness. Sometimes you need do nothing else but write down what happened, and that will be enough. In themselves, the sounds of the city can overturn what we think we know of order and causation.

This is what happens in the American poet Karl Shapiro's powerful and apparently simple poem 'Auto Wreck'. Here is part of it:

Its quick soft silver bell beating, beating,
And down the dark one ruby flare
Pushing out red light like an artery,

The ambulance at top speed floating down
Past beacons and illuminated clocks
Wings in a heavy curve, dips down,
And brakes speed, entering the crowd.
The doors leap open, emptying light;

Shapiro was born in 1913 in Baltimore, Maryland, grew up during the Depression and served in the Pacific during World War Two, writing many war poems. He said 'I write about myself, my house, my street, and my city, and not about "America", the word that is the chief enemy of modern poetry.' This is a good piece of advice for poets: to write about the things that seem small, and leave the big themes alone. Because it is in the daily specific subjects that the big themes reside.

This poem, for example, tells us a great deal about America, where the automobile was invented, whose crashes and wrecks have forced us, perhaps for the first time, to think about the question of causeless violence and death. Other kinds of death, as Shapiro says towards the end of the poem, have some kind of meaning: we know they come from illness, or war, or despair. But deaths that occur because of car accidents have no meaning. They are absurd. We have no real way of making sense of them.

In the poem, the poet looks very carefully at the auto wreck. He records the broken glass, the ponds of blood, and the wrecks that cling 'Empty husks of locusts, to iron poles'. This ardent, almost religious act of looking might be something you find difficult, but try to think of it in the context of the whole picture: you are bringing something back from the wreck (or the attack, or the accident on the metro, or the fight) that will bring further understanding to you yourself and to your reader. It isn't prurient, gratuitous looking, but a sustained, steady regard that will enable you to bear witness to what you have seen, and bring something back.

ACCIDENTS AND TRAGEDIES

The critic Roger Fry, in his book *Vision and Design* (1920), explored the difference between a tragedy and an accident. When we see an accident, we are called upon to act, to try to bring some help, call the police, alert passers-by. There is no time to think: we have to do something. But when we watch a tragedy on stage, we don't have to do anything. We can sit with our feelings as we gradually understand more about what is happening – to King Lear, Antigone, Oedipus or Macbeth.

But an accident can become a tragedy once you have left the scene and had time to collect your thoughts. Sitting on your bench by the side of the road, you might see a car knock down a skate-boarder. The car hits the skate-boarder, the boy falls to the ground, then tries to rise. He gets up, he looks unhurt. But this is only the narcosis, the illusion of unhurt that happens after a heavy blow, and soon he falls down again. You rush to the telephone to call for help, and when you sit down on your bench again you see that your hands will not stop shaking. Involuntarily, your own body has become part of the tribulation being endured by the boy and also by the driver of the car.

You have witnessed an accident and called help to the scene, but once your responsibility has ended you can survey the event as if you were witnessing a tragedy. You can reflect on the meaning of a violent action that has been caused by a mistake and which has joined you, a witness, with the suffering of both the victim and the perpetrator. Thus, an accident (even if you were yourself involved) may become the subject of the poem's gentle investigation. Because there is nothing that is not susceptible to the healing probes of the poetic imagination, nothing that will not reveal deeper meanings under the light of the poem's compassionate gaze.

Whatever presents itself for you to write about, whether it is the peaceable flocking of pigeons in a square or an argument between a man and a woman at the end of a road, listen for the rhythms of the city in your poem; the relentless rhythms of its traffic, for example, punctuated by sudden uncanny silences. Let the city deliver its rhythms through the stresses of your words, the beginnings and endings of your lines, the pauses between your voices. Be aware that the silences in your poems are just as important as your words. What you don't say leads the reader to come to their own conclusions, and the pauses, like rests in music, enable the music and the meaning of your words to sink in more deeply.

Now write your poem, with the working title 'The Sounds of ...' (insert the name of your city). Your title will no doubt change when the poem is written, but in poetry, as in prose, it is as well to place your controlling idea or controlling feeling at the top of your paper, so you can hold yourself to it, and so hold your reader still in the contemplation of your sounds.

After you have finished your first draft, read it through and then put it away in a new folder, marked 'City Poems'.

Before we leave this theme of the sounds and accidents of the city, take a look at 'Bob in Distress', from Joyce Goldstein's poem sequence entitled 'From the Upper West Side'.

Bob In Distress

Bob is in distress
he has been the victim of police over-reaching
While running with Bella in Central Park
he stopped to give her water from the fountain
running can be stressful for her
she is a big dog
when she craves water he provides it
Nearby police blare out on their PA system
'Get the dog down'
Bob shot back 'assholes'

He was called over but told them to wait
his first priority was the health of his dog
Wearing only shorts and a ripped tee shirt
he was unable to provide identification
Within minutes three police cars,
one motorcycle, two scooters, an ambulance,
and an emergency service truck,
arrived on the scene
This non-incident did not warrant
that exaggerated response Bob says
Bella was muzzled
he was charged, handcuffed and put under arrest,
He was told that they liked his dog
but did not like him
Bob and Bella were taken separately
to the Central Park precinct house
Bella was then conveyed to the Center for Animal Control
at E 110th Street and First Avenue
Bob was locked in a holding cage
Continuing requests to make a call were denied
Escorted in handcuffs to the 25th precinct
he was strip searched and fingerprinted
He was to be held overnight,
charges still unspecified
Bob was released several hours later
left standing in what appeared to be
a threatening neighbourhood
wearing only running shorts.
He ran half a mile to the CAC
to get Bella out of dog jail
He needed forty dollars and a photo of her
as proof of ownership
He was allowed to make a call
his building super came to the rescue
with money and needed items
Bob, his super and Bella walked from East Harlem
south to 97th Street as no cross town cabs would take the dog
They arrived home safely
All this for a veritable non-incident
Bob will be taking legal action

This poem is an answer to Robert Lowell's question, 'Why not say what happened?' It is anti-poetic, it uses no poetic techniques, apparently. There are no metaphors – or are there? Perhaps the whole episode, witnessed and written in bare simplicity, is a metaphor for something about America, something we may not really like to consider, something petty and cruel. Goldstein doesn't bother with punctuation – or does she? Her line endings control the reader's breathing, control the way we read and therefore how we see the incident.

She doesn't divide the poem into separate verses: what is the effect of this, do you think? It causes the reader to have to take in the full episode all of a piece. We are not allowed to select: we have to take the full measure of Bob's distress, even though it is written in a dry, distant, ironic tone.

From Goldstein's poem, you'll see that *everything* you do in your poem has a significance: your metaphors, or lack of them; your punctuation, or lack of it; your lineation (the way you begin and end your lines); and your stanza breaks (the way you divide your poem into different moments, or not). Your poetic choices are many, and though you may not be aware of them while you are writing your first draft, it's good to bring them into consciousness now so you can strengthen and reinforce them when you come to look at the poem again.

THE CITY'S SECRET TIMES

Cities have their own ingenious times and rhythms, and if you keep to certain hours you might not be aware of some of the activities that take place when you are not there. The aim of this section is to surprise you with some of the things that go on in your absence, and for you to write a poem with the working title 'When I wasn't there', which will pay tribute to the immense energy and activity of the city.

Let your poem be a psalm, an ancient form that has no fixed rhyme or rhythm but which is characterized by the presence of antiphony. This means that the poet says something one way in one verse, and then finds another way of saying it in the next. As if two choirs were singing to each other from opposite ends of a cathedral. The effect of antiphony is to increase the feeling of fullness and praise by piling up sights, sounds, images and metaphors – overwhelming the reader with sensory information. If the reader is also a singer, then participating in the singing or chanting of a psalm will increase the effect even further. One of the effects of chanting, after all, is to bring about enchantment.

Here is one of the most well-known psalms, often delivered in song.

Psalm 137

By the rivers of Babylon, there we sat down, yea, we wept, when we remembered Zion.

We hanged our harps upon the willow in the midst thereof.

For there they that carried us away captive required of us a song; and they that wasted us required of us mirth, saying, sing us one of the songs of Zion.

How shall we sing the Lord's song in a strange land?

If I forget thee, O Jerusalem, let my right hand forget her cunning.

If I do not remember thee, let my tongue cleave to the roof of my mouth;
if I prefer not Jerusalem above my chief joy.

Remember, O Lord, the children of Edom in the day of Jerusalem; who
said, Raze it, raze it, even to the foundation thereof.

O daughter of Babylon, who art to be destroyed; happy shall he be, that
rewardeth thee as thou hast served us.

Happy shall he be, that taketh and dasheth thy little ones against the
stones.

This, in my opinion, is one of the most powerful of the Psalms, full of grief
and longing and the planning of revenge. It's no wonder that it's been
adapted for song many times and has made the record industry a great deal of
money.

Note the way the lament is structured around two cities, Zion and Babylon,
with Zion, the good city, being the place where the psalmist is not. I have
mentioned this before, I know. The holy city, the good place, is always,
somehow, somewhere else.

I was once in hospital in the beautiful Galician city of La Coruña. Sunlight
streamed through my window every morning and my ward looked out on a
wide sweep of bay. I thought that there couldn't be anywhere more lovely, and
that my recovery would no doubt be quicker there than in dirty, cold, grey old
London. Then a nurse came in who spoke English. She told me how much she
missed the Holloway Road in London! Well, there you go. The Holloway Road
may be a long fume-filled corridor of a road, but someone in Spain loved it and
looked back on it with longing. Consider this as you write your own antiphon:
you might want to compare the place you are describing with somewhere else.
This will give an added dimension to the 'When I wasn't there' of your working
title.

Now for the research on your poem. Think about the times when you are
normally indoors (at work, at home, in bed sleeping), and ask yourself 'When
is the time I want to find out about?' Make a pact with yourself to be free at that
time, and set aside an hour for the same process of watching and listening that
you have carried out when researching earlier poems. Getting to know a new
time in your city is like meeting a new person: you ask questions of it tactfully;
you listen to what it has to tell you; you breathe it in to get a sense of what it is
like deep down; you notice how its textures are different from those at the times
you know, and how its colours are more vibrant or more monochrome. You
open yourself to this new time. You take it in.

As cities can be dangerous places, make sure you have taken steps to protect yourself if you go out in the middle of the night. Tell someone where you are going, and carry an alarm and a mobile phone. For the Spanish, *la madrugada*, the early hours, can be a time of jubilation, of dancing, or of eating cakes in one of the bars that stays open until all hours. But in England this time of night can be threatening. So be careful. You needn't go far from home. All you need to do is to give yourself the opportunity for this new experience.

When you have been there and become acquainted with this new time of day or night, come home and sit down in the place where you usually write. How was your city different? How did you yourself feel? Did you feel like another person as you walked around at this unaccustomed time? Did you encounter anything – a person, a bird or an animal? What was the light like? Note down your responses to these and any other questions that present themselves to you.

Then rest. Let it all sink in.

When you are ready, write the first draft of your poem. And as usual, when you've written it and read it through, don't do anything to it. Put it away in your city file. We'll come back to it later.

THE CITY'S BOASTS

There are many wonderful things about cities, glories and wonders to which we are sometimes blind because we pass them every day and they have ceased to make any impact. But poetry enables us to remember and re-live the wonder of seeing something for the first time. This next poem is an exercise in wonder.

Take something your city is proud of. You yourself might think it's a bit old fashioned, but your city prides itself on having this building/institution/park or whatever. Make a special journey to see it and, when you arrive, just sit near it and let your mind wander. Where does it take you? What does it make you think of? Wherever it takes you in your mind, follow the thread and note it all down. As a model for what I have in mind, I would like to show you a poem by Amarjit Chandan, a Punjabi poet who now writes in English.

London Eye

The London Eye can see even in the dark –
My London – a small cave in a corner of planet earth.

Over there
We sat on a bench wondering together
How I opened my heart in a breath
I am still in her parting embrace

In that park a new flower blossomed on my family tree.

Those roads showed the way
    to me – a lost outsider.

There lies my *murshid* teacher
    with books under his head
He is awake in his perpetual dream.

See the smoke rising of burning *roti* Bread of my Sorrows
and the Thames flowing from the eye.

The London Eye sees all
even in the dark.

The London Eye, the huge ferris wheel that towers over the south bank of the River Thames near Waterloo, has enabled the poet to see a long way. In a city which was not at first his own, he's been able to find his way again, connect with his teacher and see the burning *roti*, which causes tears to flow, symbolized by the Thames flowing from its own eye. Real rivers and rivers of tears; real eyes and the ferris wheel that is called 'The Eye'. Everything can stand for something else in the act of remembering, the gathering-together of lost or dismembered fragments that is inevitable when you set about writing a poem.

So let yourself dream. Something upon which the city prides itself will take you deep into the caves and passageways of your own memory, and if you follow the thread of your thoughts, you'll emerge, in the poem, with something that will astonish even you.

When you've completed your first draft, read it and put it away, and then think about this poem about Manhattan by Judy Gahagan, part of which I've included here:

Up and Down in Man-a-hat-ta (Man-a-hat-ta: Indian name meaning Heavenly Land)

It was the huge plug of granite
rooting down like a wisdom tooth
fixed that up-roar of skyscrapers;
the granite of the Man-a-hat-ta
and the invention of the elevator
back in 1857;

marooned now on the high floors
of the 1990s, where vertigo is common,
high winds may shift glass shafts
a quarter of an inch or more, cold
watercolours shiver in the strong
heroic light.

Braced shafts sustain the breathless
verticality, the sheer nerve of sliver
buildings, the purity of their glass;
but they start to outgrow the early promise;
spiritual, seemingly neurasthenic, bored,
intestine-less;

and anorexia nervosa often alternates
with bulimia: below their bony structures
the rich clefts of the streets are oozing
with stuffs to stuff the heavy soul of us,
then purging sales and riddance to rise
above the binge.

Deeper in the granite where they first cut
the railroads, where ebullient foliage plunges,
some New Yorkers live in old Algonquin caves;
you see them from the train commuting, see them
pally in their crevices, a sun shaft warming
their listless chores ...

One old man dressed in ancient black,
black pressed suit, black hat, black
careful gloves, picks bottles from the trash can,
and with his handkerchief he polishes them
to take to the distant 5-cent restitution.
He has no shoes on.

They say the earth will restitute itself too
eventually, but in the meantime (and I wish
I were about five-hundred years younger) old granite waits.
Today under dark cloud and blackish rain,
black granite, black rain, black man
are infinitely patient.

But let us not forget how lovely they are
(or will have been), all the tall buildings:
shimmying at each other, self-absorbedly
reflecting one another and the clouds
held in the sheer glass falls from heaven
above the Man-a-hat-ta.

Judy Gahagan, Crossing No Man's Land *(Flambard Press, 1999)*

Judy's original name was Judy Romany, and there's a sense, running through her poems, of wandering, and the love of moving between places. Here in this poem she is in present-day Manhattan, but imagining the ancient past of the city, and how it might be again once the city belongs to the past and the earth has restored itself.

THE CITY AS A BODY

Can you see, too, the way the city becomes a metaphor for the human body in the poem? The plug of granite that fixes the skyscrapers in place is 'like a wisdom tooth'; the skyscrapers themselves are anorexics, and underneath the surface of the city is a bulging bulimia, where the past 'stuffs the heavy soul of us', still present 'in old Algonquin caves'. Manhattan is a symbol of the great cycle of consumption and waste, a cycle that also imprints itself on human bodies in societies where there is both too much and too little of everything, in the eating disorders of their young men and women.

Consider, now, the city as a body. Where is its heart? What pumps its blood around? What are its veins? Where is its head, its centre of decision-making? What are the legs that move it along? Its arms, that make and do things? Its fists, with which it defends itself? Its liver and kidneys, that do the cleansing? Its sexual parts? Its back-passages? Where are its eyes and ears and nose and mouth? Its navel, its *omphalos* or sacred centre, that joins it to the source of its own power? What *is* the source of its power?

The city can be a metaphor for the human body, and the human body can be a metaphor for the city. Whichever way you approach it, you'll find your mind leading you in unexpected directions. Let it. The metaphor is amazingly rich and will yield some surprising material.

And when you've written your first draft of 'The City As a Body', read it and put it away in your city file.

THE BACK STREETS OF THE SOUL

The other side of the city's boasts, the aspects it's proud of and glad to be associated with, is the city's dark side, the side we find ugly or unfathomable, corrupt or impossible to live in. And if, as I suspect, everything is connected by metaphor with everything else, then these unacceptable parts are linked with the unacceptable parts of our own selves. So from both points of view, it's useful to explore them.

It's a good idea for poets to look at things that they dread, because looking brings greater understanding and greater acceptance, and so breaks up our over-simple, dualistic view of the world as right and wrong, good and bad. If we refuse to look at certain things, we can discover nothing about them: they remain in the heart's hidden chambers, liable to leap out at us when we don't expect them and don't know what to make of them. They return to us in a form we cannot understand, perhaps as haunting fantasies, perhaps as nightmares.

Looking and writing bathes the dreaded back streets in the healing light of poetry. If we look at *anything* for long enough, we begin to see it through the eyes of love, even though we might have begun looking at it through the eyes of hate, or fear.

So, consider a part of your own city that you would rather not think about. Here are a couple of poems that will help to steady your thoughts. The first is, like the previous poem, by Judy Gahagan. This time she focuses on a European city, exploring some of its ancient secrets, the things her young companion would rather ignore, rather pretend weren't there. Architects and city planners have often tried to clear away these things.

If you look at Victorian maps of London, you will see that on some maps many streets are painted black. Even though these streets were often just behind main thoroughfares, their black colouring meant that they were dangerous, and respectable people shouldn't go there. They were ruled by pimps and prostitutes and were where you could see 'penny gaffs' (public outdoor sex shows), and have a 'tuppeny stand-up' (sex standing up in an alleyway for tuppence). They were streets of terrible destitution and despair, the despair we all experience at some time in our lives if we are honest and clear with ourselves.

Martina Evans' poem looks at the Holloway Road, the long, horrible, fume-filled corridor I spoke of earlier, and turns it into an object of delight and wonder. Can you do this, do you think, with an unacceptable part of your own city?

Impatient To Move On

And when we finally reached the town at dusk
it was swaddled in fog. We groped past *Hotel de* this
and *Hotel de* that, they'd been *Hotels-Dieu*, it seemed,
now closed, straitjacketed in their blackened timbers.

Perhaps you imagined plague spores in their cellars
Or that they, narrow-faced and pitiless with dogma,
had watched peasant girls dragged out for burning,
for you were frightened of the town: 'Let's move on!'

For being young your dream is, like Le Corbusier's,
of disease-free happy garden cities, with clean
light-filled houses, of his beacons of optimism.

But I believe that in the back streets of the soul
there is a medieval zone of cramped interiors;
I sense the meanness of its sour old women,
steep gables of piety, catatonic inconvenience.

As we took the road leading out across ramparts
to pass grey watchtowers, clammy with fog-sweat,
I glimpsed a last window positively blaspheming
light: a hair salon where exuberant young girls
were robed in red, draped in blood-red towels,
reforming obscurantist hair, impatient to move on.

Judy Gahagan, Crossing No Man's Land

In Celebration of Holloway

To the Half Moon
The Crown,
and The Devonshire Castle.

To the Sea Chef,
with their fish in tank and crumb,
their Cypriot chips.

To MacDonalds
where I've heard jailbirds speak.

To the No.43 bus that brings us
one way to The Little Angel Theatre,
the other way to the Rainbow Toyshop.

To the apple blossom so quick,
the Irish and the Greek.

To the West Indian reggae
beating out of cars and windows.

To the majestic Sikh who guards
the door of the newsagents.

To Wet and Wild where you can buy
the sound of the sea in a whorl
for one seventy five.

To the green and blue view
from our high camera windows.

To the mini cab driver whose car
broke off in pieces in my hand.

To the moss growing in the pavements,
the dandelions in Manor Gardens.

To the fool who wrote SEX on a lamp post.

Martina Evans, Can Dentists be Trusted? *(Anvil Press, 2004)*

Now go to this place that you dislike, that the city should be ashamed of. Go in broad daylight with a friend if it is a truly dangerous part, and note down, neutrally, without judgement, everything you notice. What gives it its life, do you think? How does it keep going? Try to put your own dislikes aside, and see it from the place's point of view. What part does it play in the life of the city as a whole? Why is it still in existence? Because if it wasn't performing some important function, however small, however unacceptable, it would surely have been cleared away by now.

Have as a working title 'The Bit I Hate' and, when you're ready, write your first draft. Then read it and put it away.

In the purely gratuitous arts, poetry, painting, music, our century [the twentieth century] has no need, I believe, to be ashamed of its achievements, and in its fabrication of purely utile and functional articles like airplanes, dams, surgical instruments, it surpasses any previous age. But whenever it attempts to combine the gratuitous with the utile, to fabricate something which shall be both functional and beautiful, it fails utterly. No previous age has created anything so hideous as the average modern automobile, lampshade, or building, whether domestic or public. What could be more terrifying than a modern office building? It seems to be saying to the white-collar slaves who work in it: 'For labor in this age, the human body is much more complicated than it need be: you would do better and be happier if it were simplified.'

W.H. Auden, 'The Poet and the City', in *The Dyer's Hand* (Random House Inc., USA, 1962)

IMAGINARY CITIES

For your last poem in this chapter, I want you to imagine your ideal city. Would it be a 'beacon of optimism', as in Judy Gahagan's poem, one of those 'disease-free happy garden cities, with clean/light-filled houses'? Or will there be room for dark places in your city, the places worthy citizens don't always want to acknowledge? How will your city celebrate its heroes and heroines? With statues? With park benches? With trees? And how will your citizens move from one place to another? Where will they live? And how? Alone? In families, or in other kinds of groups? What will the workplaces be like, and the spaces where your citizens spend their leisure?

There are endless questions you can ask and answer, and remember you are starting from scratch. Your city can be exactly as you want it to be. It is your own city.

Before you start your poem, take a look at 'Gunachaur', another poem by Amarjit Chandan.

GUNACHAUR

I have never been to Gunachaur.
When I hear the word Gunachaur
    something happens to me.

Mother used to talk about her distant relations
      living in Gunachaur.
I used to fly there on her wings.

I felt –
    Gunachaur is a place
    Somewhere beyond Jalandhar
      Near Nawan Shahar.
    A light flickers in darkness seen from above.
I imagined the relations I never met.

Even now that place is not far off
It's near   quite near
Where ever I happen to be
My mother is with me
    And Gunachaur is close by.

Gunachaur isn't an ideal city. It's a city the poet has never visited, but it has a life inside him because it was alive as a memory for his mother. In his mind it is tangled up with early memories of her and, because of this, it is often nearby, as she is. Gunachaur isn't an imaginary city either: it's an emblem of the power of the imagination to evoke a place that was loved by someone whom the poet loved, and still loves. It's an imaginary city even though it is at the same time real, because it has its life within the heart of the imagination, and within the heart. Your own imaginary city may be of this sort.

Now write your poem.

Read it, and put it away.

REVIEW: LISTENING TO THE RHYTHMS OF YOUR CITIES

When you go through the poems you have written in this chapter, I want you to concentrate on their rhythms and whether the rhythm underlines and emphasizes what it is you want to say.

To begin with, ask yourself how fast or how slowly you want this poem to move. Should it creep up on the reader slowly, or should it zip along like a young girl on a Lambretta? The iambic metre (one TWO, one TWO, one TWO) will keep it at a steady walking pace, whereas the trochaic metre (ONE two, ONE two, ONE two) will make it burst forth with the energy of running.

It is most likely that your poems will not abide by any regular metre, but if you indicate, above each syllable as you go through them, where are the strong beats and where the weak, you'll be able to see where the high points are in each line, and ascertain whether they come where you want them to come.

Every line has its own climax, and so does every verse. You want to slow your reader down at these points, centre them in reverie so they think deeply about this moment in your poem. You can do this by using the spondee, two stressed syllables, which pulls the movement of the poem to a temporary halt, and also by using long vowels (ah, oh, ee, uu) and words that begin with vowels, which slow down the rhythm of the line or verse to something relaxed and dreamlike.

When you want the poem to speed up, then you can use lots of consonants or even some alliteration ('Peter Piper picked a peck of perfect pickled peppers'). Alliteration makes the poem gallop along, whereas assonance (repeated vowels) and consonance (vowels that sound similar) slow it down.

You, the writer, are in charge of the pace at which the reader moves through your poem. You speed your readers up or slow them down according to the inner landscape of the poem. Moving along the city streets you might want your reader to move fast, whereas when contemplating an accident you may want to hold everything still. Arriving at a monument, or one of the dark back-streets, on the other hand, you might want to slow the reader down with an iambic metre and plenty of assonance and consonance.

So use this review to consider the rhythm of your poems, and use the ways I have indicated to control your poem's tempo. A poem that moves too fast will cause the reader to miss its meaning. A poem that moves too slowly will cause the reader to lose concentration.

Timing is crucial.

6 FREE VERSE OR GIVEN FORMS OF POETRY?

W henever you're in a quandary over whether your poem should run free or become itself through the form of, say, a sonnet or a pantoum, rest assured that this quandary has existed for a long time, and poets have always argued (with one another and with themselves) over what will best suit their own poetry.

John Milton preferred blank verse: ten syllables in each line, but unrhyming. In his preface to *Paradise Lost* (1667), he wrote about 'the troublesome and modern bondage of rhyming ... Rhyme being no necessary adjunct or true ornament of poem or good verse, in longer works especially, but the invention of a barbarous age to set off wretched matter and lame metre.'

John Dryden makes the contrary argument. In his preface to his verse play *The Rival Ladies* (1664), he writes: 'Imagination in a poet is a faculty so wild and lawless that, like a high-ranging spaniel, it must have clogs tied to it, lest it outrun the judgment. The great ease of blank verse renders the poet too luxuriant.'

The French essayist, Michel de Montaigne, said 'Even constancy is a more sluggish form of movement' and we could argue, analogously, that even free verse is a kind of form. Not a form that is imposed from the outside, but one that involves listening for the inner music of the poem, the melody, rhythm, tempo, timbre, counterpoint and lineation that will give the poem its fullest power.

But how do we get to the poem's inner music, as that music seems to make itself felt in different ways, depending on our time and on our place? I think, for the American poet Robert Frost, blank verse and the iambic line felt so natural that, when we read his poems, we are often beguiled into thinking that it's just ordinary talk put into lines to look like a poem. Look, for example, at part of 'Mending Wall', one of his most well-loved poems:

There where it is we do not need the wall:
He is all pine and I am apple orchard.
My apple trees will never get across
And eat the cones under his pines, I tell him.
He only says, 'Good fences make good neighbours.'

The story of the poem lies in the apple farmer (Frost himself) and his neighbour walking along the length of the wall that divides their farms after the 'frozen-ground-swell' of winter, repairing the holes that have appeared with stones that fit, and talking a little as they go along. That's all. It seems, from that account, a very minor anecdotal poem. And yet Frost renders it all with such limpid simplicity, such a low, easy voice (he rarely raises his voice in any of the poems) that the words begin to resonate in the reader's mind as a metaphor for something very important: the questions of how much we need boundaries between ourselves, and what boundaries do to protect us and keep us neighbourly with one another.

Frost doesn't always write in blank verse. He is a master of rhyme: there is really very little he can't do with his poems. So why did he choose blank verse for 'Mending Wall'? I think it was because blank verse was as near as Frost could get to complete freedom at the time. He may have railed against free verse, but that was because form was where he found his freedom, and blank verse was the freest of all the forms at his disposal. Free verse existed, but Frost didn't feel easy with it, and so his poems emerged in different permutations of rhyme and metre.

And how are you yourself to decide, when a poem beckons you, whether it would feel easier in free verse or in a fixed form?

THE INTEGRITY OF THE LINE

Poems aren't just bits of prose split up into lines of different lengths (I seem to remember that the poet Stevie Smith said that they could be, but I suspect she was lying): each line has its own reason for being its own particular length. Look at this poem by the American modernist E.E. Cummings, written in the same half-century as 'Mending Wall':

> plato told
>
> him:he couldn't
> believe it(jesus
>
> told him;he
> wouldn't believe
> it)lao
>
> tsze
> certainly told
> him,and general
> (yes
>
> mam)
> sherman;

and even
(believe it
or

not)you
told him:i told
him;we told him
(he didn't believe it,no

sir)it took
a nipponized bit of
the old sixth

avenue
el;in the top of his head:to tell

him

Frost and Cummings were writing in the same country at roughly the same time, but their ways of writing could hardly be more different. Frost defers to the forms, while Cummings is concerned to break them apart. Frost the quiet, conservative farmer (though I think he was what the Americans call an 'ornery critter', a difficult animal) and Cummings the trickster, the breaker of convention: does the way we write lines depend, then, mainly on the poet's own personality?

Well, let's experiment with that idea. After all, the two poems aren't so very different thematically. Frost is exploring the question of human boundaries, of whether or how much we need them, whereas cummings is trying out the problem of how much we can learn from other people, if anything: whether we have to be whacked on the head by a piece of metal (the 'el' refers to the elevated train tracks above the city) before anything finally sinks in. Do the two poems really require such radically different lineation, ways of ordering their lines?

Try the problem out in two poems of your own. First, explore 'Boundaries', then 'How do we learn things?' in whatever form comes to you: quatrains, blank verse, free verse, the sonnet, whatever.

Listen quietly until your first line comes to you. Does it come as a ten syllable line, or much longer, or much shorter? Trust the poem to tell you what it wants to say in the way it wants to say it. Remember that the poem is coming to you as an idea, a sensation, a feeling – or as a phrase, already burgeoning into a form of words. Your job is to listen intently, deep inside the tent of the poem's own privacy, until it emerges in its entirety.

At first, the words may well come out quite jumbled, not seeming to make much sense. No matter. Say them out loud to yourself to hear how they sound in the air first. You'll quickly hear the words that sound wrong, and you'll find they've dropped away when you say the poem again.

This is what the Russian poet Osip Mandelstam described as cutting away the dead wood. The poem might come to you encased in its own fluffy, punky, dead-wood protective covering, but as you stay with it, that will begin to fall away, revealing its own naked beauty. The poem might not want to reveal itself all at once, so be patient.

When you feel you have enough (twenty words perhaps) to make a start on paper, write it out in full lines. This will help you to catch what the poem wants to say to you, in prose at first. It may well say much more as you revise it, but the first draft gives you a clear foundation: this is the basis of the poem's music and meaning. Because with poems, the music and the meaning often come together: the rhythm of a phrase, the lifting or falling melody of a particular form of words. Write down as much of it as comes to you this first time around, then sit back and look at it.

Now read it out loud.

Listen to your breathing. Where do you pause to take a breath? This will give you a clue about where to break your lines. A line in poetry has its own integrity, its own wholeness, and the places you want to take a breath may well be where you want to end a line. Because when you don't have line endings imposed on you (if you're writing a sonnet or terza rima, for example, you have to have around ten syllables in every line) you have to listen for when the line *wants* to end. It's more difficult. But it's also much closer to daily speech, and so you begin to hear the music that lies hidden away in ordinary words. So it can be much more satisfying, too.

The poet Ted Hughes, in his book of essays called *Winter Pollen: Occasional Prose* (Faber & Faber, 1994), made the analogy between poetry and hunting. He said he began to write poems when he stopped hunting: a lying in wait for the needed form of words, and getting them down on paper as a kind of capture. For me it isn't quite like that, although I can see what he meant, and perhaps every poet has their own metaphor for how a poem arrives. I think W.H. Auden said that at the beginning of his writing life he would be hanging around on street corners waiting for poems.

For me, it's the act of listening that's paramount. The poem comes to me, sometimes insistently, demanding that I write the first draft straight away, or hesitantly, hovering, making itself felt more and more strongly over several days. The poem is a new being in my life. I might welcome it, or I might resent it at first. A new being requires time and attention. It means that other obligations, arrangements, habits, need to be pushed out of the way to accommodate it. You must be sure never to feel guilty or selfish about this. Poems have just as much right to exist as people or theories or newspapers or conflicts – more, perhaps. Because poems, although in the beginning they may just seem to be stirring up trouble, always end by bringing about release, resolution and reconciliation, of whatever was causing the trouble in the first place. So never feel bad about giving them plenty of standing room.

There is, in fact, a world of poetry indistinguishable from the world in which we live, or, I ought to say, no doubt, from the world in which we shall come to live, since what makes the poet the potent figure that he is ... is that he creates the world to which we turn incessantly and without knowing it and that he gives to life the supreme fictions without which we are unable to conceive of it ...

The deepening need for words to express our thoughts and feelings which, we are sure, are all the truth that we shall ever experience, having no illusions, makes us listen to words when we hear them, loving them and feeling them, makes us search the sound of them, for a finality, a perfection, an unalterable vibration, which it is only within the power of the acutest poet to give them. Those of us who may have been thinking of the path of poetry, those who understand that words are thoughts and not only our own thoughts but the thoughts of men and women ignorant of what it is that they are thinking, must be conscious of this: that, above everything else, poetry is words; and that words, above everything else, are, in poetry, sounds.

Wallace Stevens, from 'The Noble Rider and the Sound of Words', from *The Necessary Angel* (Alfred A. Knopf, USA, 1942)

But how, when poems are allowed their own freedom, should you arrange them on the page? How can you be sure you are giving the poem the shape it wants?

Take a look at these two versions of a poem called 'Jealousy' by the London poet Sheila Hillier. I asked the writing group to try this subject using long lines, because I suspected that breaking the barrier of ten syllables in a line might free the poets to probe deeply into their own experience, and allow metaphors to emerge that would put the readers in touch with their own uncomfortable feelings of jealousy. In probing our wounds, it's sometimes possible to get behind them into sources of power that are solid and eternal, that lie beyond the haunted habits of our present personality.

This is Sheila Hillier's first version.

Jealousy

You can go blind with watching, or lose the connection
of brain and eye so even inanimate things
start to move round in complicated ways,
make sounds like bellows or punctured bladders thrown from a height.

The smallest things matter,
there is a black white-headed bug in my house and
    whether he's skating the slats of the
Venetian blind

falling into the red folds of the carpet
or simply sauntering across the bathroom tiles,
   he knows more than I.

My fingers separate the blind so I can peer
at the hard glare of the world
The bug sees sunlight striped across my face,
   turning me zebra.

The bug rolls up into a mottled bead, he's specially coated, thin and
   flexible
with soft parts but no blood
   and so I flick him on the floor ...
Someone who's cut the letter Y in me
from belly to neck
is opening up the flaps to take a look.

But when it's over and the membranes
are stretched out and dried,
   each organ has been weighed,
and residues are rinsed away, I feel a stateliness.

Then I can say

go out under a big sky
   look as far as you can.
Perhaps the sun will vaporize the aromatic oils of your head
and bleach your yellow hair.

And I can stop
   digging out my shadow.

You can see that the long lines have allowed the metaphors to come out: the white-headed bug that has entered the house, that 'knows more than I'; the cut, in the shape of a letter Y (Why?) into the narrator of the poem, so that her insides are visible for 'Someone ... to take a look.'

But do the emphases fall in the right place, so the reader can really enter into the pain of jealousy through the poem? Enter it in a measured way, so that it does not completely overwhelm, but allows the reader to see it, experience it, discover something from it, and then emerge, free? Perhaps not. Some of the lines are so long that we are asked to take in too much at once. Perhaps the poet needs to impose some sort of pattern, so that the experience can emerge slowly, in a more overtly ordered way. Perhaps she needs to more thoroughly control the experience of the reader.

William Wordsworth believed that were two forces at work in a poem: first, the 'spontaneous overflow of powerful feeling,' the urgency that causes the poem to be written. And second, 'emotion recollected in tranquillity' which is the ordering, naming force that enables both poet and reader to make sense of the powerful feeling. Sheila Hillier has the first in this version of the poem, but does she have the second, yet?

She evidently didn't think so, because she came up with another version:

Jealousy

I can go blind with watching or lose
the connection of brain and eye

so even inanimate things start to move round
in complicated ways, make sounds like

bellows or punctured bladders thrown from a height.
The smallest things matter. There is a black

white-headed bug in my house and whether he's
skating the slats of the Venetian blind falling

into the red folds of the carpet or just sauntering
across the bathroom tiles he knows more than I.

My fingers separate the blind so I can peer
at the hard glare of the world.

The bug sees sunlight striped across my face,
turning me zebra. The bug rolls up into

a mottled bead, he's specially coated thin and flexible,
bloodless with soft parts and so I flick him on the floor ...

Someone who's cut the letter Y in me
from belly to neck is opening up the flaps to take a look.

But when it's over and the membranes are stretched out
and dried, each organ has been weighed and

residues are rinsed away, I feel a stateliness.
Then I can say: go out under a big sky

look as far as you can. Perhaps the sun will
vaporize the aromatic oils of your head,

bleach your yellow hair. And I can stop
digging out my shadow.

Read it on the page and then read it out loud. Does it feel different to the first version? What's the effect, do you think, of ordering the poem into couplets? Does it make it go faster or slower? Do you feel you have more control, or less?

For me, the second poem makes me move more slowly through the emotion, because the poet gives me the opportunity to breathe. I have the line-endings to pause in, and the punctuation within the lines. I also feel I have more control, because I see the predictability of couplets ahead, and I don't have to negotiate my way through a wild sea of tossing stanzas. I can therefore concentrate on allowing the poem to help me explore the feeling of jealousy.

And that's the key: to find a form that supports the feeling rather than distracts from it. The first version was too complicated, too fussy even. In the second, the poet has found the form that will help the poem and then disappear into the background, rather than drawing any unnecessary attention to itself. In the second version, too, because the movement is slower and less hectic, I can really believe in the lovely liberating moment in the final stanza:

And I can stop
digging out my shadow.

This ending is so good that the reader needs to come to it slowly, to feel the inevitability of it after the terrible display of anxiety and human insides, the gut-wrenching of earlier on.

Can you feel where the poem turns and begins to lift itself out of the slough of jealousy? I think it comes in the tenth stanza, the one that begins 'But when it's over ...' You'll see that Sheila Hillier has changed some of the lines here, too, so the reader gets a discrete thought all together, rather than broken up. You may also notice that this, the beginning of the resolution, comes roughly two thirds of the way through the poem, as it does in an Italian sonnet, and similar to the way that a landscape painting is often divided into two-thirds sky, one-third ground. It seems that there's something intrinsically satisfying about this shape, which is called the golden mean or the golden section, and signifies harmony or the mid-point between extremities.

RHYTHM IN FREE VERSE

Just as a line contains its own intrinsic wholeness, which will reveal itself when the poet listens with full attention, so the rhythm of the line, the rhythm it needs so it can do its own mysterious business fully, will emerge when the poet says it over and over, so that its own powerful beats can make themselves felt. And, as with line endings, it's the line's *own* rhythm, rather than any imposed from outside, that's important here.

In the ancient past, poems were composed in formal metre because they were frequently associated with dance. Poems could be chanted to the accompaniment of the lyre, Apollo's stringed instrument – lyric verse, causing enchantment – or danced to the accompaniment of a drum, causing an uprising of courage or warlike feelings. You can remember metrical verse more easily (and rhyme aids memory, too – those suffering from Alzheimer's disease can sing songs long after they have lost all other obvious connection with language). Some of the poems were very long, designed to occupy the endless hours of television-free evenings. So everything that helped you remember was a good thing.

Nowadays, the ancient conditions rarely apply. You sit at home or in a library holding the poem in your hands, or you hear the poet read his or her work at a poetry reading. Some poets do recite, rather than read, their own work, and the eye-contact and immediacy that occur when this happens give the poems a special intensity. But nevertheless writing has changed the way we approach poems: we don't need or expect to learn the poem by heart, so we don't absolutely require the rhymes or regular metres that help us remember them. The poems are free, now, to appear in their own rhythm.

So how do we discover this rhythm? Take a look at this poem, by the London poet Maureen Li. It's called 'The Wall Fell Down the Day He Died' and the poet is writing about her husband, who was living away from her when she heard about his death.

The Wall Fell Down the Day He Died

Afterwards, after she'd heard
she put down the phone, turned to the garden
but a violent gust had flung the wall
out across the frozen beds

crumbs of mortar scattered
the soft yellow bricks fallen apart like puzzled friends
but still lined up
holding on to the memory of a wall.

Later she had it built again
bricks tracked down all over London
so you couldn't tell the new ones from the old.
The paving stone under the rowan
where he stood sometimes of an evening
stayed split in two.

Once she saw him, clear as day
in the sweater she'd knitted, walking towards her
along some street, head down into the wind.

121

> After that it stopped: those glimpses
> just before waking
> by the hedge in the last of the light
> in the mirror, turning away.

What I want you to do is to mark, on the poem, where are the strong and where are the weak beats. Put a horizontal line over the syllable where you feel an emphasis falls, and a little 'v' mark above the weaker beats.

Can you see that an emphasis falls on the first syllable of 'Afterwards', and on the following 'after' also, and then, in the third line, on the first syllable of 'violent,' and also on 'gust'? These rhythmic emphases, because they come so often in the first stanza, give us a sense of the uncanny surrounding his death, the way the elements seem to join in celebrating it. In the first stanza there are four strong beats in every line, with few weak syllables in between. The poet is holding us still, slowing everything down with her stresses, so we can't look anywhere else but at what the knowledge of his death has done to the wind, and what the wind has done to the wall.

Can you see that here, too, as in Sheila Hillier's poem, there is a turn after line fourteen, exactly two thirds of the way through, and that the final stanza marks a clear appearance of the lost one, and then a gradual slipping away? Maureen wrote to me that this turn was difficult for her.

> I did have trouble with the first three lines of the last stanza – kept
> rearranging it. Then I suddenly remembered that day in Betterton Street.
> Walter was wearing a black sweater I made for him when we were first
> together, and with that new phrase it fell into place.

There it is again, that waiting. Maureen kept moving the poem around and feeling it wasn't right – and then the memory returned to her that enabled her to complete it. The words with their appropriate rhythms will come when you are able to give the necessary attention to the poem. It has been waiting a long time for you to get round to it, in all probability. Time for you now to give it the attention it needs. Not the filing, the paying of bills, the 'essential' telephone call: the poem, your deeper need, requires attention first.

Note, also, the way the rhythm changes in the very last four lines, moving down from four beats in a line (the rhythm of ballads and narrative poetry) to three or even two beats. As the appearances diminish, so do the number of stresses, until we are left with silence, completion. The dead one has come to say goodbye, powered by all the force of the elements, and then returned to the land of the dead, clothed in the familiar sweater, the poet's gift to him.

THE WAY THE POEM COMES TO YOU

The American poet Marilyn Hacker wrote about Ezra Pound's advice to young poets to 'break the back of the pentameter', in other words to break the hold of the always-popular ten syllable line. When I asked one of the poetry groups to write a poem with very long lines, then, I was curious to see how the poets experienced the wildness of long lines without rhyme. One, an English poet called Sylvia Rowbottom, came up with this mysterious poem that seemed to emerge straight from the depths of sleep. Here's what she said about how the poem came to her:

> In this poem, my aim was to sustain the oddness of the first line which was in my mind when I awoke one morning, though not part of a dream. Also, being a long line, it seemed an opportunity to write a long-lined poem.
>
> I anticipated that the stars would predominate, but they were immediately overwhelmed by the nets. Nets seem to me to be an extraordinary progression in human development, as useful to humans as shells to crustacea, say, and as finely wrought. Fragile, deadly, huge, air-framed, essential in some areas to our survival. An evolutionary tool.
>
> The sun came in through the door to exaggerate the boatman's movements and lighten up the (I felt) claustrophobic effect of the net-shed. Also to lift the poem.
>
> I wanted the boatman's disposal of the stars to show as a habitual action which always fascinated him, also to indicate in their swim 'for the sky' that they were real stars – for the whole incident to be commonplace until fractionally caught in the pitiless searchlight of dreams.

And here is the poem itself:

Checking the Thread

> 'The world at a distance is best' said the boatman, prising a star from
>   his net,
> travelling it up between finger and thumb to rest on a ledge with the
>   others.
>
> No sound in his movement, the nets took all noise to themselves,
> muffling into their delicate lattice the undisturbed hubbub of years.
> Sweeping over the boatman's knees and my knees, layering the warm
>   boards
> waistdeep in places, swooping up walls, rooting at oak studs struck in at
>   differing levels,
> hammocking under the roof. Only the door and the floor swing clear.

He raised the first fold on his nails. Yard after yard rode his finger-ends,
bright in the door-light, sun squinting and blinking, crazy with
    chequered joy,
netting his lighted face, leaping and swerving, joking the walls.
Manweb, threaded air tesserae, fluid as seawater, smelling of life before
    death.

'This one's done.' He lowered the heavy folds down and stood up.
Freeing his feet, he swept the stars into the cup of one hand and
carefully stepped to the door, raised the cup and flung the stars clear of
    the wall.
They swung up and down in the sea's oily lap, then turned like a little
    flotilla
and swam for the sky.

He watched, forgotten hand curved at his neck, as he always did,
to see what the stars did.

What feeling do you get from a poem of such long lines? They seem to me to contain their own air of mystery, conjuring slowly the boatman with his amazing nets, nets that seem to hold the whole world. Had the lines been shorter, they would have been more manageable, easier to comprehend. But Sylvia has perhaps allowed them to run to these lengths precisely so that we could not fathom them so easily.

Everything seems big in this poem. Is the boatman God, creating new parts of the world? Or a sort of grim reaper, gathering together lives just before they die? Whatever he is, he overflows the lines, and perhaps even overflows the whole poem, leaving us wondering about the massive part he seems to play, in creation and also in the end and transformation of lives.

In Sylvia's poem, the long lines are surely exactly right. If you try breaking them up, the effect is entirely different: the poem loses that overwhelming quality that the opening line clearly requires. In maintaining the long lines all the way through, the poet has been faithful to the spirit or essence of the poem.

And it's this spirit or essence that is your surest guide when you are listening for how the poem should be. Perhaps, like Sylvia, the first line will come to you. If it does, you are lucky, because the length of it will indicate the length of the rest of your lines. They tend to come together, as short or long, depending on the images and ideas the poem wants to convey. But always be open to a line of a different length: sometimes a very short line wants to stand on its own in a long-lined poem, bringing the reader up short – as if the short line is itself a mark of punctuation, inviting the reader to pause and let the poem as it is so far sink in more deeply. And sometimes the opposite will happen: a long line will importune you in the middle of short-lined stanzas. Again, let it come. It has asked to be there for a reason. You may not know why at first, but you will after a time. Perhaps an image needed to luxuriate, to spread itself out, or perhaps a complex thought needed more room to breathe. There will always be a good reason for the necessary length of the line.

Lineation has to do with breath, with short breaths or long breaths. As you work on your poem, walk around the room saying it out loud. Does it want you to take small breaths frequently? If it does, it wants short lines. Or does it want you to fill your lungs with oxygen and let out your breath slowly, allowing the words to fall drop by drop, pearls, or seawater, staining the breadth of the page? If so, let the words roll from the left- to the right-hand margin. Don't try to rein them in. Let them roll.

DECIDING ON STANZA LENGTH

How do you decide where your verses should begin and end, whether they should be long, or short, or of differing lengths? Well, remember that *verse* is from the Latin for *furrow*, and that *stanza* is from the Italian for *room*. You are ploughing one furrow at a time, or moving from room to room. But what is a furrow, or a room, a metaphor for, do you think? Look back at your own poems, to see how you have instinctively made the breaks. And look again at 'Checking the Thread' to see where Sylvia's made them.

If a line-break signifies the break of a breath, or a short pause before one line tumbles into the next, a verse break means something more. You are moving your reader on from one moment, one image, or one idea, to the next. It's not so different, really, from the change from paragraph to paragraph in a piece of prose. You have completed one thought, so you move on to the next one, signalling the change with the necessary space.

How would you define the different moments in 'Checking the Thread'? For me they go something like this:

Verse One: Introduces the main idea of the poem: the boatman and the nets.

Verse Two: More about the nets.

Verse Three: The meaning of the nets: life before death.

Verse Four: The stars.

Verse Five: The boatman again, watching.

Can you see how each verse of the poem approaches its core subject from a different angle, taking us deeper and deeper into the metaphor of the nets?

And what do the nets mean to you? For me, they stand for creation, with the boatman himself a creator, some kind of negotiator between life and death. He is an ancient symbol, and water a powerful archetype for the crossover between this world and whatever may follow – but the nets introduce a new element, 'seeping over the boatman's knees and my knees', holding everything together in a mysterious yet playful way.

ENDING YOUR POEM

How do you know when your poem is complete, that it's said fully what it wanted to say? How do you avoid going too far, so the reader feels you're bashing them over the head; or not far enough, leaving the reader feeling at sea, with the nagging question: 'Now, what was that all about?'

Firstly, remember the poet Basil Bunting's famous saying: 'Never forget that the reader is at least as smart as you are.' So never explain, patronize or lecture. Overstatement of whatever kind always puts your reader off. Your reader is your equal, and your own best beloved: someone who will willingly follow the thoughts and images in your poem, and be led to the conclusion you want them to come to. Trust your reader to follow you to the end.

Secondly, trust the poem to let you know when it wants to end. Don't worry yourself with thoughts like 'But have I really said enough?' If you've walked around the room saying the poem into the air, you will come to feel when it has achieved its completion. And the more poems you have tested out in this way, the more sure your instincts will become about the sense of an ending.

And thirdly, give yourself the freedom to *play* with the end of the poem, as Sylvia has done here. The poem, in a way, follows Aristotle's classic narrative shape for all art: verse one is the opening; verse two, the development; verse three, the climax; verse four, the turning-point; and verse five the *denouement*, or untying of the knots.

Really, the poem could end at the climax, at the lovely line at the end of verse three, which ends 'smelling of life before death'. But Sylvia then turned it, to tell us more about the stars, and then rounded it off in verse five with a final portrait of the boatman. She turned the poem back upon itself, so we could see the boatman 'at a distance', just as he advised us to look at the world when the poem began.

You might like to consider Aristotle's narrative shape, to see if your own poems have already been following it unconsciously. The structure is so deeply written inside us that it is already part of our unconscious world, one of the forces that shape everything, from the smallest anecdote we tell, to Hollywood films, to Greek tragedy. So you may be curious to see whether some of your poems follow it. Here it is in a little more detail.

The Opening: where we discover the situation of the work of art. The spring about to uncoil.

Development: where we learn more about the life of the people and places that inhabit the work. This may also give us a clue as to why the original situation has occurred.

Climax: where the drama is highest, and the work seems to achieve its highest tension.

Turning-point: where the action takes an unexpected turn. We begin to learn the other side of the drama. This would coincide with line nine in an Italian sonnet, where the resolution begins.

Denouement: where all the knots, the mysteries, are finally revealed. In one of Shakespeare's sonnets, this would take place at line 13 and 14, where he suddenly lets go of the tension that's built up in the first twelve lines.

You may find that some of your own poems accord with Aristotle's structure, and, if they do, this may help you to recognize more surely when they have reached their ending.

BREATHING YOUR POEMS

But whether they follow Aristotle's, or their own shape, your poems will respond to being breathed. Their inspiration came from inside you. It was through you that they first appeared on the page. You breathed in your world through your sensations and experiences: your poems are a way of breathing out, of giving the world back to itself in a transformed way. And you can test the power of a poem by reading it again, to test whether the breaths come in the right place, whether you have paused appropriately at the end of the lines and the end of verses, giving the poem itself room to breathe, to have a life of its own.

The more you breathe your poems in this way, the more they will become part of you, and you will begin to find that you know some of them by heart. This is a good sign, because the ones that are committed most easily to memory are the ones that resonate with your mind and body – and if they resonate with you, the chances are that they will also strike a chord with other people, your (as yet) unknown audience, which is out there waiting. The poet Wallace Stevens said 'You can't get the news from poems, but men die every day for lack of what is found there.' Many people in the world are waiting and longing for poems. Your next task is to find those who are specifically waiting for your own work.

7 GETTING YOUR POEMS OUT INTO THE WORLD

You now have a folder of poems, some of which you may be happy with, some you may see as exercise pieces. How has your attitude towards them changed as you worked your way through this book? Some people say, when they are beginning to write poems, that they are doing it only for themselves. But that tends to change as the writing develops. You begin to see yourself as part of a community of poets, and become curious about what your peers are writing. This is where the poetry magazines come in, because they are where you can look at other people's work and they can look at yours.

Charlie Chaplin said to the poet Hart Crane that poetry is 'a love-letter to the world', to which Crane replied: 'A very small world.' Whether the world is small or large, the writing of poems makes it bigger, and you will find that, the more you write, the more the world is prised open by your poems, so that, finally, everything becomes poetry. Poetry sacralizes the world, returns it to its source, which is infinite, the origin of everything that is made and everything that is not yet made.

Up to now, your poems have existed only in your own private realm, and that is as it should be: they emerge out of the dark, from the unknown recesses of the unconscious. But now it's time to go public. Poems want to be aired, to be known, to be spoken. They bring to the surface things that were hidden before. So it's not a smart move to hide them.

The first thing you need to do now is to let people know what you have been doing. Writing poems isn't an activity that should be kept secret. Your friends and family should be told that you have not been down the bookies, or tramping around the shops. You've been involved in one of the most important activities known to humankind: re-enchanting the world. If others are to be persuaded to join in the action (of changing the scene from one of depressing profit and loss to one suffused with beauty, terror and wonder), then you have to come out of the closet and reveal what you've been up to.

How do you do this?

Stick your haiku on the fridge, on wardrobes, on toilet doors down the pub.

Make your own poetry graffiti and stick it to whatever surface comes to hand.

Stand up and recite one of your poems at a party.

Stop buying birthday and Christmas cards. Make your own instead. Write a special poem for each friend.

Put your poems in e-mails, on postcards, on phone messages.

Don't write letters, write poems.

POETRY MAGAZINES

When you find you want to reach a wider audience, beyond your own friends, work colleagues or family, you will begin to investigate the world of poetry magazines. I interviewed the editors of some of the stronger, better-established poetry and art magazines to find out from them what kind of work they do, what they want to achieve, and what they are up against in the busy marketplace of letters.

First I spoke with Laurie Smith, one of the editors of *Magma*. You can find out more about this magazine by looking at their website (www. magmapoetry.com). *Magma* originated in 1994 out of a poetry class at the City Literary Institute run by Laurie himself. A group of editors emerged from the class. They didn't research the poetry scene beforehand to discover whether there was 'a gap in the market', as a commercial concern would have. They simply wanted to publish what interested them – poems that were true to their feelings, and well-made too.

At first, *Magma* survived entirely on sales and subscriptions. Laurie says he remembers that the editors had to prop it up with some of their own money, but it was printed at Kings College at first, where Laurie also worked, so the work was done cheaply, at cost price.

Magma is unusual in that it is published by a committee of editors, with a rotating main editor for each issue. It comes out three times a year, in summer, autumn and winter, and the fact that there are between eight and ten people involved means that responsibilities and burdens can be shared. In their editorial, they say:

> *Magma* is unusual in being run by a small group rather than an individual. Several writers with a roughly similar view of poetry got together and shared out the tasks. They decided that each issue should have a different editor but, for continuity, each editor is advised by the editors of the previous and subsequent issue. The strength of the rotating editorship is that each editor brings his/her particular interests to bear, resulting in poems and emphases that no one else in the group could have predicted. We feel that this arrangement works because we have a similar idea of what makes a good poem.

As I write, *Magma* is preparing issue number 30, which will have a theme of mental health and mental illness, a tenth anniversary edition. Arts Council funding came in 2003, enabling the magazine to be redesigned, and sales and subscriptions are looking very healthy.

A Shiver Round the Room

One of the places where *Magma* is sold is at poetry readings. These are held (one for each issue) at the Troubadour Poetry Café in Earl's Court, London. If your poem is published in the magazine, you will be invited to read it at one of these large poetry gatherings, hosted by the vibrant Irish poet Anne Marie Fyfe. It's a place where, when you are ready, you can gauge the power of your poem by the response of the audience. They are polite, they won't boo you off the stage as they might in some poetry slams, but you will be able to tell, by the quality of their listening and the quality of their silence, how strong an effect your poem has had.

You will be able to discover the effect of your poem by the way it resonates through your own body as you read it out to a group of strangers. Your body is a kind of echo-chamber: it will tell you how you and your poem are doing. If you listen to the room, you will be able to tell how the audience is listening to you. Their silence tells you that they are there with you, following attentively the words you have written. Movement, fidgeting, fiddling with feet and bags indicate that, however briefly, you've lost them. Take note of this, because this part of the poem you will have to look at again. If your audience loses concentration at any point in a poem, you will need to revise that part.

And if you feel a tremor in your own body, that is the best sign, because it means that a shiver has run around the room. Again, take note of that point in the poem, and underline it, because your tremor tells you that that part of the poem is particularly powerful. You can't often detect these highs and lows for yourself. An audience is one of the ways to discover them.

What You Are Up Against

It takes a good while to get your first poem published, so don't be put off by the snowdrifts of rejection slips that will come through your letterbox at first. *Magma* receives about two thousand poems per issue, and publishes about sixty. By my reckoning, that gives you a one in thirty-three chance of getting in. So the odds are steep: you are a serious outsider. But then again, you have only a one in fourteen million chance of winning the lottery, and people are always buying tickets for that. And you are being judged on the strength of your poem, not on chance. Remember that the Derby has been won by a 66 to 1 outsider, and the Grand National by an outsider of 50 to 1. If you are a good horse and you have trained on (that is, not slackened off in your craft) then you will succeed. It looks unlikely, but it is possible.

A fascinating magazine that comes out of Huddersfield is *The North*, edited by Janet Fisher and Peter Sansom. Both are well-known poets, and Peter Sansom has also written an excellent book called *Writing Poems* (Bloodaxe Books, 1994). *The North*, like *Magma*, emerged out of a poetry workshop, and Janet Fisher told me that they, too, look for poems that feel authentic, different or unusual. They can be in one of the forms or in free verse.

I think you write for a small audience, an ardent critical audience. And you know Graves says that poets ought to take in each other's washing because they're the only responsible audience. There's a danger to that – you get too specialized – but I pretty much agree that's the audience you do write for. If it gets further, that's all fine ...

You want to feel there's a certain degree of poorer writing that wouldn't get published in the magazine your work appears in. The good small magazine may publish a lot of rather dry stuff, but at least it's serious, and if it's bad it's not bad by trying to be popular and put something over on the public. It's a wrenched personal ineptitude that will get published rather than a public slickness. I think that has something to do with good reviews coming out in the magazine.

Robert Lowell *Paris Review Interview*, from *Writers at Work: The Paris Review Interviews, Second Series*, ed. Malcolm Cowley (The Paris Review Inc., 1963)

The North has a growing list of subscribers, but unlike *Magma* there are no regular poetry readings. Instead, they have a yearly competition, which invites poets to submit up to twenty pages of poems for a reasonable entry fee. The overall winner has a full collection published, and the runners-up have pamphlets. So this is a really good way of getting your work known, and a stroke of genius on the part of *The North* that helps to keep it afloat and thriving: a synthesis of enterprise and outreach that is attractive to both the publisher and the poets. More information about *The North*, and about Smith/Doorstop, the poetry press, can be found on their website (www.poetrybusiness.co.uk).

THE AND SO? TEST

Both *Magma* and *The North* are looking for poems that are authentic, different and true-to-feeling. How do you give your poems the best chance of being noticed by magazine editors? This is where the 'And So?' test comes in.

As an editor on *Ambit* magazine (more of which later), I read many poems that should have moved me to laughter, deep thought, or tears. They didn't, because they didn't pass the 'And So?' test.

The 'And So?' test says: OK, so your mother's died/your uncle abused you/you had a near-death experience/your partner cheated on you. And so? I hear about these things all the time, the newspapers and airwaves are full of them. How has your poem made the subject any different, any more arresting, than the thousand other times I have read about it?

Simply describing the subject doesn't necessarily give your poem the resonance it needs to make an editor notice it amid the other huge piles that come in. So first of all, look at the figurative language in your poems. Remember that everything is connected to everything else: if you can make a connection that the reader hasn't thought of before, then you're beginning to engage.

There's a poem by the American writer Theodore Roethke (pronounced 'Retkee') that describes the way his father beat him. (So, your father beat you. And so?) But he describes the beatings as a dance, and in fact calls the poem 'My Father's Waltz'. It captures the attention because at first the connection seems very strange. How is physical abuse like a dance?

Well, first of all there is the rhythm. Both hitting and dancing involve the repetition of a beat. One kind of beat is destructive, the other is life-enhancing. But they both spring from the deep rhythms of Nature: create, destroy; pleasure, pain; love, hate; breathe in, breathe out. Roethke is sublimating (making sublime) the memory of the beating into something quite different, and in doing so he causes us to see the love that can lie inherent within violence. He causes us to see further into the complexities of our lives.

Some anthropologists say that football began in the act of kicking around the head of an enemy: that it began as a response to murder and tribal violence. Whether or not this is true, we can see that the beautiful game harnesses and transforms very ancient and primitive energies. It couldn't have become a worldwide sport of such popularity and power if that weren't the case. This is also so in your own poems. You take the subjects that spring from the core of yourself (and therefore the core of every human being), and transform them through metaphor into something arresting, something so strange and beautiful that it stops the readers in their tracks.

Making a Song and Dance Out of It

How do you literally stop the reader, and how do you move them on? Remember that the ancient Greeks built their rhythms around the human body, and around the song and the dance. We can still use their methods to achieve strong but unconscious effects in the person who is hearing or reading our poems. So, for example, if you want to create a dancing rhythm, you can use the dactylic metre. Dactyl is the Greek word for finger: one long joint and two short ones. Your rhythm will go: ONE two three, ONE two three, ONE two three, and so on. Like a waltz. In free verse you vary the rhythm, you don't keep it the same all the way through, because everyday speech just isn't like that and it could get to sound old-fashioned and boring. But you can keep the ghost of the dactyl there so the reader is dancing along with you without realizing it.

Here's a rhyme to help you remember the trochee and the dactyl, told to me (to my great delight) by my grandfather, when I was a child:

Here we suffer grief and pain
Over the road they suffer the same.

The first line is trochaic (ONE two, ONE two, ONE two, ONE) and the second line dactylic (ONE two three, ONE two three, ONE). Both being energetic metres, they burst in upon the reader: they are wake-up calls.

If you want the reader to limp along slowly with you, on the other hand, you can use the metre we tried in our pilgrimage poems: the iamb. Here again, to help you remember how it works, is another verse often repeated by my grandfather, one that I imagine must have emerged from the gallows humour of the First World War.

I have no pain, dear mother, now,
But oh I am so dry.
Connect me to a brewery
And leave me there to die.

I don't know the rest of the poem, or whether there is any more to it, but the fact that there are four iambs in lines one and three, and two iambs in lines two and four, places it in the category of a ballad, the poem that tells a story to the reader, as if you were walking along slowly with the poet and they were gradually telling you what happened.

And when you want to really hold the reader still, you can use the wonderful spondee, which is two strong beats together: Stop! Look!

But always remember that in contemporary poems the rhythms of everyday speech are the wellspring, rather than any imposed metre. The trick is to allow the ghost of an ancient metre into the ordinary words, as Winston Churchill did in one of his famous speeches:

We shall fight them on the beaches ...

Can you hear the echo of the anapaest in that line (one two THREE, one two THREE, one two THREE). Churchill didn't use it slavishly, or perhaps even consciously, but just allowed it to slip into his speech, so the rhythm could root itself in the minds of those who heard it: so they couldn't get it out of their minds.

Rhythm, if used subtly, is a way of hypnotizing your readers, of enchanting them with the hints of regular metre: it is another way of making sure that your poems are true to feeling and yet formally fascinating at the same time.

FINDING OUT ABOUT THE MAGAZINES

When you can, visit the National Poetry Library (on the fifth floor of the Royal Festival Hall, near Waterloo Station in London, at present, but moving to another venue in April 2005 while the Royal Festival Hall is refurbished), or visit them on their website (www.poetrylibrary.org.uk). This will give you information about the services the library provides, including poetry events and readings, as well as the dates of poetry and literature festivals all around

> It would do no harm, as an act of correction to both prose and verse as now written, if both rime and meter, and, in the quantity of words, both sense and sound, were less in the forefront of the mind than the syllable, if the syllable, that fine creature, were more allowed to lead the harmony on ...
>
> Let me try to put it baldly. The two halves are:
>
> the HEAD, by way of the EAR, to the SYLLABLE
> the HEART, by way of the BREATH, to the LINE
>
> And the joker? That is in the 1st half of the proposition that, in composing, one lets-it-rip; and that it is in the 2nd half, surprise, it is the LINE that's the baby that gets, as the poem is getting made, the attention, the control, that it is right here, in the line, that the shaping takes place, each moment of the going ...
>
> And the threshing floor for the dance. Is it anything but the LINE? And when the line has, is, a deadness, is it not a heart which has gone lazy, is it not, suddenly, slow things, similes, say, adjectives, or such, that we are bored by? ...
>
> ... every element in an open poem (the syllable, the line, as well as the image, the sound, the sense) must be taken up as participants in the kinetic of the poem just as solidly as we are accustomed to take what we call the objects of reality; and that these elements are to be seen as creating the tensions of a poem just as totally as do those other objects create what we know as the world.
>
> **Charles Olson, 'Projective Verse', in** *Poetry New York* **magazine (1950)**

the country. It's a wonderful place to sit and read, listen to a tape of your favourite poet, and watch them perform on a video.

The Poetry Library also provides a site that you can consult to find the names and addresses of the many poetry magazines in Britain (www.poetrymagazines.org.uk). The Poetry Library has digitized the poems in most of the magazines, and is continuing to update its collection, so you can get a good idea of the kind of work different magazines publish from looking at this site. But it is still worth sending for copies if you can afford to: it's good to read an issue page by page, so you can get a feel for them and decide which magazines you yourself like and enjoy. If you feel drawn to a particular magazine, there's a greater chance that the editorial staff will like your poems – eventually anyway. You may have to experience many rejections before a magazine shows any interest. Don't be at all put off: this is the experience of most poets.

The Poetry Library also holds magazines from different parts of the world. If you would like your poetry to be published elsewhere, whether because that country is your own point of origin, or just because you want to, then it is worthwhile finding out about these publications. I myself have connections with the USA and with Australia, and have had poems published in the *minnesota review* (USA) and *HEAT* (Australia).

My Own Experience of Getting Published

When I first began working for the City Literary Institute, a writer called Carol Burns edited a magazine there called *MATRIX*. In *MATRIX* I read an article by Fred Sidgwick which described the work of some of the poetry and literary magazines. So I began to send my poems to those magazines, six at a time with a covering letter and a stamped addressed envelope, and waited for a response. Nothing. Like many poets, I lost confidence, and tried to pretend that I wasn't writing. But I was, on the quiet, and eventually I sent one poem (only one: not a wise thing to do at all) to *Ambit* magazine. Very much later – *Ambit*, like many of the magazines, is often slow to reply – I received a letter from Martin Bax, the editor, saying they would publish my poem, and that I should send some more. I was so happy I screamed, and my family thought something terrible had happened.

And, in a way, it had. When I had been published once, I was confirmed in the writing, and this made it even harder to stop. I began to have poems accepted in other magazines (*Acumen* in Devon, *The London Magazine*, *Poetry Review*, *The North*, *The Rialto*, *Magma*, more in *Ambit*) and won, and was runner-up, in a couple of poetry competitions, which resulted in the publication of two pamphlets.

But the pace of all this was incredibly slow – as slow as the love Andrew Marvell says he would devote to his coy mistress, if he had the time. I continued to write because I simply couldn't stop. Poems were my own form of creativity. I had to honour each poem when it wanted to appear, as a gardener has to honour her garden when it needs tending. I never shot to fame or achieved much success, but I loved the work. I saw it (and still do) as one of my main reasons for being alive. It's what keeps me alive, and feeling lively. Feeling in tune. Feeling in the rhythm, in the flow of life. Especially when I contracted a serious illness and had to spend time in hospital, it kept me going. Many other writers have confirmed this: poetry keeps you alive when the going gets very tough.

When my second daughter was born, I started to work for *Ambit* one day per week, at first purely on a voluntary basis. I saw all the poems and stories that came in, organized poetry readings, proofread the magazine and took it to press, motoring up to the Lavenham Press in Suffolk every three months with Martin, who took the day off from his work as a paediatrician, working with severely handicapped children.

I found out at first hand just how much work is involved in making a quarterly magazine, and conceived a great admiration for the editors who begin them, and give so much of their own time (and, often, money) to keep them going. Martin Bax and Edwin Brock (a wonderful poet who was then *Ambit*'s poetry editor) also gave me some useful advice about how they read the submissions that come in. Edwin said:

People can study all the English literature they like, but when I'm reading a pile of poems late at night, I want to be excited ...

and Martin added:

> You're sitting on the sofa reading, and if the poem hasn't hit you by line
> ten, then it won't make it. A writer can use nice forms, but it has to hit
> you.

In his work as a children's doctor, Martin often has to travel around the world
to speak at conferences and inspect hospitals. He will take a file of poems with
him to read on the plane.

> I can read three lines and then interrupt it. I'm never an editor at a desk.
> The poem has to obtrude into all the other areas. I really like poems, but I
> hate being bored.

Bear this in mind: the editors are often tired. They are reading poems in the
evening, after a day at work. They want something to wake them up. If your
poems can give that wake-up call, as if the world were in its own early
morning, fresh and new, then they stand a chance of holding the editor's
attention.

And I began to understand why it takes magazine editors so long to reply to
writers: because they are often doing the work in their spare time, after they
get home from being a teacher, or a doctor, or whatever their day-job is. They
read your poems as soon as they can, work and general exhaustion permitting.
So give them two or three months to get back to you, and if you have heard
nothing by then, contact them again. Write and tell them when you sent your
poems to them and ask when you can expect their decision. Your letter will
usually hurry things along.

Remember that many rejections will come through your letter-box. Poetry is
rather like ancient Greek boxing: the longer you can bear to stand up getting
hit, the greater will be your chance of emerging the victor in the end. So keep
yourself in good shape, both mentally and physically; find other ways of
keeping up your self-esteem when the poetry is going badly. But most of all,
keep writing. There's no other way to improve. A haiku a day when your
strength is low, to keep your hand in. Sonnets for when you want to work on
problems and solutions. Pantoums for when certain thoughts obsess you,
going round and round in your head. And free verse for when poetry pours out
of you, in rhythms and melodies that refuse to be confined in traditional metre.

A MAGAZINE FOR YOUNG PEOPLE

The poet Ted Hughes wondered why young poets, who showed such talent and
promise in the W.H. Smith Young Writers' Competition, generally did not
mature into adult writers. He concluded that the imagination needs exercise,
that it atrophies if it's not used. I believe that many young writers, like adults,
also need outlets for their work: they want it to be read by a wider circle.

As I write, a young editor called Kate Pemberton (who is also the assistant editor for *AMBIT* magazine) is attempting to launch a magazine for seven- to fourteen-year-olds, called *Avalanche*. It will include fiction, art, poetry and reviews, and the emphasis is on the off-beat, the wild. It will be the first magazine in Britain to publish only the work of that age-group, and will try to encourage the readers to participate by including features such as a blank page entitled 'This Page Is For You' and 'Be Inspired', with ideas about what to try in writing. Kate herself was inspired by an American magazine called *Stone Soup*, also for young people, which has been going for thirty years and has 30,000 readers.

I hope very much that *Avalanche* will work and give young writers the encouragement and energy they need to keep going. If you want to see the quality of the work that will go into it, here's a poem by Kyriacos Soteris, from Enfield, Middlesex (aged eight when he wrote this).

BAD DOG

I cried to her
I fried for her I lied to her just to get a
Dog to sit on a log I made
For it I call him
BAD DOG
she said yes I play
chess with him. now I had him for a
month I taught him tricks like to eat wicks.
you give him champagne he'll
drive a crane or crash a
plane he's a leaky dribbler he is so
bad he will drink from a – the sink
he eats ink you won't like his
angry blink that's
BAD DOG

If you want to find out more about *Avalanche*, including whether it has indeed taken off to function as a quarterly magazine, you can contact them by e-mail (avalanche-magazine.co.uk). And if someone (7–14, remember) sends them a poem and doesn't hear within a month, then they should try again. Kate is avoiding rejection slips by keying in poems she wants on the computer directly they come in, and letting poets know very quickly when their work has been accepted; she only notifies those whose work has been accepted. I think this is a brilliant way to respond to new poems: perhaps the grown-up magazines should start using it, too.

POETRY IN MOTION

If none of the existing poetry magazines interests you, or if you live in an area where there are no poetry events, what are you to do? You have to start your own. The poet Philip Larkin said that he wrote what he did because no one else seemed to be writing it, and the founder of The Crowood Press (which has published this book) is reported to have begun publishing because no one else was printing the books he wanted to read. Nature abhors a vacuum. So if you find one, fill it.

First, you need to get together with other people who want to make, perform and publish poems. How do you do this? You can find some adult education classes and join a writing group, you can put notices in your local libraries, doctors' waiting rooms, hospitals, and make announcements on local radio stations. People will come once the word is out.

Then decide what you want to do. Perhaps you will just read your work to one another at first, using the feedback you get to help you revise your poems. After a while, you might want to put on a performance, hiring a room above a pub and bringing in some musicians and singers too, to give variety and a change of pace.

Eventually you might sell pamphlets of your work at these poetry events – produced on the computer or designed with the help a local print shop. Many poets have begun in this way. The point is to get your work known around the local community. And then, if the poems go down well, you may find yourself being asked to read or perform at larger events, further afield, as the word gets round.

GOING SOLO

But if you want to work alone, then you will have to rely on the existing poetry magazines to get you started. Send a selection of six poems, along with a stamped addressed envelope. (Some magazines accept e-mail submissions, but not all do, so it is important to check beforehand.) Include a covering letter which lists the poems that you are sending in, and if you have had work published before, remember to mention that fact. Sometimes this can persuade the editor to look a little more curiously at your poems.

GIVING YOUR POEMS THE BREATH OF LIFE

Finally though, even the most shy poets are tempted out of the closet to perform their work. When you decide to go public, make sure your mind and your body are fit and flexible enough to take the strain.

Check out the venue beforehand. You need to know how your own body, mind and voice will fit into it. If it's vast, echoey and hall-like, you will need to grow a little. If it is small, you stay the same size. But whatever the size, atmosphere or acoustic, you want to fill the space, so your own voice hits the far wall, embraces your audience, and then comes back to you. To do this you can work on your breathing until you can speak longer and longer portions of your poem in one breath.

Your head, your vocal cords, your lungs, indeed your whole body, are musical instruments which you can prepare and tune to give your poems their most powerful effects. In yoga, breathing from the diaphragm is considered the most effective both for achieving calmness and for activating the full range of the voice. So prepare yourself by pulling in your abdomen, then allowing your diaphragm and your whole chest, including the top part up by your shoulderblades, to fill up with air. Feel the air even filling the parts round the back, behind your waist.

You'll notice, after a few of these breaths, that you are feeling simultaneously relaxed and energized. This is the state of mind you want to create and maintain while you're reading your poems, because states of mind are contagious, and this is how you want your audience to feel: relaxed and alert, patient and eager, calm and wide awake. This is the best state for listening to poems as well as for reading them.

Next, work on increasing the resonance, the echo-quality, of your voice, by practising certain sounds to clear the passages in your head. Humming 'mmmmm' sounds will clear the front, 'nnnnnn' will clear the middle, and 'nnnng' the back. The Barefoot Doctor, writing in *The Observer Magazine*, says that humming these sounds will also improve sinus headaches and help get rid of a hangover.

To increase the range of tunefulness in your voice, its ability to move very high and very low, as well as through the middle ranges, practise choosing a sound ('ahhhh', for example) and singing it from beneath your boots to over the top of your head, from deep bass to coloratura soprano. Imagine the sound moving slowly up your body and floating just below the ceiling.

Then practise bouncing different sounds off the walls: 'eeeeeee', 'oooooooh', 'ooooooo', 'ayyyyyyy', 'bbbbbbb', 'ccccccc', and so on. You will begin to feel your voice return to you, as a boomerang does after it has reached its target. And you will begin to really like the sound of your own voice: most important, because if you do, your audience will too. Use only about half the power of your voice when you are practising. It's crucial not to strain your vocal cords. Let them get stronger slowly and treat them with care so as not to damage them.

INTERNATIONAL WRITING

All the poetry magazines in Britain welcome poems from writers of different cultural backgrounds, but some particularly concentrate on international writing. One of these is *Wasafiri*. This literary magazine, founded in 1984, aims to 'create a definitive forum for the voices of new writers' and it describes itself as 'Britain's only international magazine for Black British, African, Asian and Caribbean literatures.' *Wasafiri* includes articles on topics such as translation and Trinidadian writing. You can find out more about the magazine on their website (www.wasafiri.org).

If you are from a culture which might be described as outside the mainstream and you have something you want to say as a poet, it is vitally important that you don't keep your light hidden. Western culture is changing all the time, and is crying out to hear the voices that bring a new knowledge, a deeper and wider understanding of how we live, take delight, suffer, and how we die, too. So even if you think that a magazine looks a bit old fashioned, a bit stuffy perhaps, send them your poems anyway.

KEEPING GOING

As you continue to write, you will discover more and more about your gifts as a poet. As you develop your capacity to listen more intently, different poems will come to you, sometimes from layers of yourself that you weren't aware of before, sometimes from parts of the world, its material and spiritual dimensions, that are entirely new to you. Let them come. Refuse nothing. Poems are our first inklings of new realities. How are they going to find physical form if the poet is resistant, or always attending to something else? Animals might speak to you, or angels, or blades of grass, or even bin liners. Listen, always listen. Get it down. You are the midwife to the new world that is waiting, that is trying to be born.

GLOSSARY

Alliteration   A repetition of consonants to give a sense of quickness to a poem, or to create a strong rhythm. You find them in the children's chants 'Peter Piper picked a peck of perfect pickled peppers' and 'She sells sea shells by the sea shore'. Another example is the opening of Longfellow's poem Hiawatha: 'By the shores of Gitchee Goomee/By the shining Big Sea Water ...' (*see* Chapter 5).

Antiphony   The calling of one voice to another in a poem or a song, as in a psalm (*see* Chapter 5).

Aphorism   A short, arresting, saying, similar to a proverb (*see* Chapter 3).

Assonance   The repetition of vowels in a poem, which often has the effect of slowing the reader down. A famous example is Keats' 'Thou still unravished bride of quietness,/Thou foster child of silence and slow time.' It takes longer to enunciate a vowel, either out loud or in the mind, than a consonant, so the reader has to decelerate (*see* Chapter 5).

Ballad   A poem that tells a story, often in four line or six line verses, with three or four stresses in a line. Ballads usually rhyme. Examples include 'La Belle Dame Sans Merci' by John Keats and 'The Ballad of Reading Gaol' by Oscar Wilde.

Blank verse   Ten syllables in a line, unrhyming. *See* Chapter Six, on free and fixed forms.

Consonance   Where similar-sounding vowel sounds are repeated. As with assonance, this slows the reader down.

Counterpoint   In music, this means 'note against note'. In poems, it is where two or more voices work against one another, creating a fugue. It is an attempt to thicken the texture of language, perhaps causing the reader to see something from several different points of view.

Couplet   A verse of two lines, either rhyming or unrhyming.

Dramatic irony   Where something is revealed to the reader, in a poem or a play, that the speaker involved is unaware of. A famous example is the Duke in Robert Browning's 'My Last Duchess', who is not aware of his own cruelty and sadism. *See* the section on Agamemnon in Chapter 4.

Dramatic monologue   A poem written from a particular character's point of view (*see* Chapter 4).

End-stopping   Where the sense of the sentence ends at the end of the lines, as in Dylan Thomas' famous villanelle 'Do Not Go Gentle Into That Goodnight'.

Do not go gentle into that goodnight.
Old men should burn and rage at close of day.
Rage, rage against the dying of the light.

Enjambement   Where the sense of the sentence runs on from one line to the next, for example in Shakespeare's sonnet:

Let me not to the marriage of true minds
Admit impediment ...

Feminine ending   When a word ends on an unstressed syllable. *See* Chapter 2, the section on terza rima.

Free verse   Sometimes called Vers Libre, which is French for Free Verse. Here the poem has no fixed form. There are no fixed number of syllables, no regular metre and no rhyme.

Glose   A Spanish verse form that takes four lines from an existing poem as the epigraph for a new poem, and then integrates these four lines at the verse-endings of the new poem (*see* Chapter 3).

Japanese verse   No rhyme or regular metre. The basic unit is the syllable, which is why it has inspired many contemporary poets. See particularly the work of the American poet Gary Snyder. *See* Chapter 2 for a discussion of haiku, tanka, renga and haibun, which are the major forms.

Kyrielle   A verse form based on the repetitions of the Mass: 'Lord have mercy and Christ have mercy'. Rhyming or unrhyming four-line verses, with every verse having the same last line, as a kind of refrain.

Lineation   A study of the way a poem begins and ends its lines (*see* Chapter 6).

Masculine ending   When a word ends on a stressed syllable (*see* Chapter 2).

Metre   A group of syllables, long and short, or stressed and unstressed, that defines the rhythm of a poem. The main metres are: the iambic metre (one TWO, one TWO, one TWO); the trochaic metre (ONE two, ONE two, ONE two); the dactylic metre (ONE two three, ONE two three, ONE two three); the anapaestic metre (one two THREE, one two THREE, one two THREE); the spondaic metre (ONE TWO, ONE TWO); and the pyrrhic metre (one two, one two – all unstressed). One iamb, trochee, etc. is called one metrical foot. I imagine they are called feet because they were originally part of a dance.

Octave   The first eight lines of a sonnet, where the poem's 'problem' is often explored (*see* Chapter 3).

Pantoum   A poem in quatrains, originating from the Far East. Lines two and four of verse one become lines one and three of verse two. Lines two and four of verse two become lines one and three of verse three, and so on. *See* Chapter 3 for an example of this.

Prosody   A study of the forms, diction and syntax of poetry: versification. From the Greek, to sing.

Quatrain   A verse of four lines, rhyming or unrhyming.

Rubaiyat   The plural of 'rubai' – a Middle Eastern verse form, in quatrains, with ten syllables in each line and a rhyme scheme 'aaba ccdc eefe gghg' and so on. Can be any length.

Sestet   The last six lines of a sonnet, where the resolution is often explored (*see* Chapter 3).

Sestina   A verse form consisting of six and a half verses, where the last words in the lines are repeated in a different order in each verse (*see* Chapter 3).

Sonnet   A poem of fourteen lines, with ten syllables in each line and varying rhyme schemes. Can also be unrhyming (*see* Chapter 3).

Syllable   One beat. For example, my own name, Julia Casterton, contains six syllables: Ju(1) li(2) a(3) Cas(4) ter(5) ton(6). Usually consists of one vowel with a consonant on either side.

Tempo   The speed at which a poem moves.

Tercet   A verse of three lines, either rhyming or unrhyming.

Terza rima   A poem in tercets, with ten syllables in each line and a rhyme scheme 'aba, bcb, cdc, ded, efe', and so on. Can be any length. Dante invented this form for his *Divine Comedy* (*see* Chapter 2).

Timbre   The quality of sound in a poem. Whether the poem is quiet and private or rousing and public, as if it were being played by a full orchestra or a brass band.

Villanelle   This verse form, originating in Provence, means 'farm work song'. It has six verses, with ten syllables to each line. Lines one and three are repeated alternately at the end of each verse. They also end the sixth verse. Verses one to five have three lines, and verse six has four. The most famous examples are Dylan Thomas' 'Do Not Go Gentle Into That Goodnight' and Elizabeth Bishop's 'The Art of Losing Isn't Hard to Master'.

Volta   The 'turn' in a sonnet, which usually comes around line nine, where the poet begins to see the other side of the picture (*see* Chapter 3).

Waka   An ancient Japanese form. Each poem has thirty-one syllables: five in the first line, seven in the second, five in the third, seven in the fourth and seven in the fifth. This is also another word for tanka, described in Chapter 2.

INDEX